W9-CUF-182

A Boy's Guide to Life

THE COMPLETE INSTRUCTIONS

From The Editors of Planet Dexter

Illustrated by Bob Staake

PLANET DEXTER®

A Satellite of Addison Wesley Longman

Copyright © 1998 Real Life Publishing
Illustrations copyright © 1997 Bob Staake

ISBN 0-201-15168-5

Cover design by Chris Sykes
Book design by Marta Rulifson, MKR Design
Illustrations by Bob Staake
Text set in 10-point Bureau Grotesque by Vicki L. Hochstedler

1 2 3 4 5 6 7 8 9 -RNT-0100999897
First printing, October 1997

Through the Addison Wesley Longman Triangle program, Planet Dexter
books are available from your bookseller at special discounts for bulk
purchases; or, contact the Corporate, Government, and Special Sales
Department at Addison Wesley Longman, One Jacob Way, Reading, MA
01867; or call (800) 238-9682.

And Now a Message from Our Corporate Lawyer:

Neither the publisher nor the author shall be liable for any damage that
may be caused or sustained as a result of any of the activities in this book
without specifically following instructions, conducting the activities without
proper supervision, or ignoring the cautions contained in this book.

You can find out more about the Planet Dexter family at:
http://www.planetdexter.com

The Planet Dexter Guarantee!

If for any reason you are not satisfied with this book, please send a note
telling us why (how else will we be able to make our future books better?), along with the book, to The Editors of Planet Dexter, One Jacob
Way, Reading, MA 01867. We'll read your note carefully, and send back to
you a free copy of another Planet Dexter book. And we'll keep doing that
until we find just the right Planet Dexter book for you.

CONTENTS

CONTENTS
BY CHAPTER

Around-the-House How-To's 77

Cool Things to Make 86

Paper Cutting..98

Printmaking and Painting 107

Things to Do Indoors............................113

Games for Groups.............................114

It's in the Cards 128

Introduction

Thanks for choosing to read *A Boy's Guide to Life*. We all hope you enjoy it and that it gives you lots of good ideas about fun and useful things you can do to make your own life more interesting.

Here's how we found all the stuff in this book: we asked hundreds of kids (and grown-ups) for things they knew that they thought other kids ought to know. Some of them sent us their ideas by e-mail, some by regular mail and some even telephoned us. Sometimes, the information came from parents and teachers, but a lot of it came from kids just like you. We've tried to identify everybody who helped us by making a list of contributors. You'll find it at the back of this book.

If you know something you think other boys ought to know, please send it to us. We'll include it in our newsletter or use it in another edition of this Guide.

Our address is:

Kids Life
116 W. Jefferson Street,
Mankato, KS 66956 USA

Or you can visit us on the World Wide Web at:
http://www.kidslife.com

Either way, we hope you'll stay in touch with us—and with all the other kids who made this book possible.

Thanks!

P. S. The publisher enjoys hearing from kids, too—really! You can write them at:

The Editors of Planet Dexter
One Jacob Way
Reading, MA 01867

Or you can send e-mail to:
pdexter@awl.com

1

Money

Money is how grown-ups keep score in a game that doesn't always mean very much. Real "money" is a handshake from a friend or a hug from a grandma. That's a better way to keep score in a game that means everything. So what is money good for? Well, money is fun to make because it shows how well you meet responsibilities while still having fun and making up great ideas. Here are some ideas for making money.

Chores for Cash

A lot of these ideas are oldies-but-goodies—people will pay to have these chores done!

Snow Shoveling

Form a team of boys and go door to door. The more boys, the faster you'll complete the job; the faster you complete the job, the more jobs you can take on; the more jobs you take on, the more $$ you make! You should have road salt as well as shovels, as part of your gear.

Raking Yards

People hate raking yards. You can get rich doing it for them. Here's all you need: a rake and some leaves.

Washing Cars

If you get a crew, it will be easier, but you'll also have to share the money with your helpers. You decide.

■ Make sure all the windows are closed before you hose the car down.

■ Soap the car down by hand, using rags or big sponges. Always start at the top and work your way down. When your bucket of soapy water gets too dirty, be sure to dump it out and replace it. Don't forget the tires—they collect a lot of dirt.

■ Rinse the car off thoroughly with the hose. Dry it well with rags.

Vacation Specialist

Let people know you're available to take in their mail and water their plants when they're on vacation.

KiDS' SUGGESTiONS

We asked kids to tell us what they did to make money and here is some of what they said:

"Charge money if you and your friends are going to have a big game of football. Charge 25 cents and put out some chairs. Have a game every Saturday."

"At my library I found a book called Better Than a Lemonade Stand. *It's full of great ideas on how to make money. Plus, it's by a teen, not some adult. My friend and I are going to start one of the businesses in the book, but they all sound fun."*

"Hi! I am a kid who started a business with a good friend. We walk dogs for a very low price."

"I found out last year that lemonade stands make a lot of money. I charged $.25 and made $17.00 (Hint: Sell lemonade on hot days. Sell in the morning so people will buy lemonade on the way to work. Also keep a lot of ice, napkins and paper cups on hand. Have a place to keep the money you made.) Good Luck!!"

TO GET A SOCIAL SECURITY CARD

Call the Social Security Administration at 1-800-772-1213.

More Ways to Make Money

Start a Collection Museum

First, you'll need to find a space to set up your collection museum. See if one of your friends—or a neighbor—will donate an empty garage or shed for a week or two. Once you've found your space, have every kid with a collection bring it to the museum. Get some card tables and set the collections up on them. One person can be the "curator," and keep track of the collections. The curator also handles the money and decides which collection should go where. Have each collector write a statement about his collection, and place it on a wall nearby.

Once the collections are properly set up, get ready to open up your museum. Place fliers around your school and neighborhood, announcing the museum's opening. Also, put an advertisement in the school paper—or even the local paper, if it isn't too expensive. Charge a reasonable entrance fee and get friends, neighbors, and parents to visit. (Contributors get in free, of course.)

At the end of the exhibit, divide the money you made equally among the contributors.

Lemonade Stand

Who doesn't like lemonade on a hot day? If you use a frozen concentrate, jazz up the pitcher by floating a couple of slices of lemon on top. Keep your ice in another container so you don't dilute your lemonade.

Helping Grown-ups Get on the Internet

If you are good at computers, put notices up around the neighborhood that you're available to help in this area. Many adults are intimidated by computers and will happily pay to have someone show them how to do some of the basic stuff, like how to get on-line, how to send and receive e-mail, and things like that.

Toy Auction

Gather up all the old toys you and your friends are tired of. (Get your parents' okay, though.) Give each person a receipt for each toy.

1. Pick a date and give the auction lots of publicity. Put up posters.

2. On the day of the auction, put all the toys on display. Give everyone a chance to look over the merchandise. Now you're ready for the auction.

3. Stand on a box or chair and start the bidding. All bids should start with a quarter. Be a creative auctioneer—the more you talk up the toys you're selling, the more money you'll make.

4. Write the final selling price of each toy on the receipts . As the auctioneer, your take is 10%. Make sure you keep accurate records.

What to Do with the Dough

Saving Money

When you deposit money in a savings account, you're letting the bank use your money for loans and investments. In return, the bank pays you interest. If you're thinking of putting your money in a savings account, be sure to shop around for the bank that gives you the best interest rate. The interest rate is always a percentage—as a rule, the higher the percentage, the more money you'll earn. If the interest rate is four percent, for example, that means you'll earn four pennies for every dollar you have in your account.

In addition to finding out the interest rate, you'll also want to know how often the interest is *credited,* or added, to your account. This can be monthly, yearly, or somewhere in between. It can vary from bank to bank. The more frequently interest is credited, the more money you'll earn from your account. Of course, the more money you save, the more interest you'll get, too.

Some banks charge you money if you don't deposit regularly and others have a penalty for making a withdrawal. Find out the bank's rules before you open an account.

What's Compound Interest?

When the interest on your money starts earning its own interest, that's called compound interest. Here's how it works: say you have $1,000 in your savings account. If your compound interest rate is five percent, in 15 years you'll have $2,080. The higher your compound interest rate, the more money you'll save—and more quickly, too.

THE RULE OF 72

There's a well-known formula for figuring out how long it will take to double your savings account money. It's called the "Rule of 72." Divide the number 72 by your interest rate—the number you get is your answer.

For example, suppose your interest rate is six percent. Divide the number 72 by 6 and you get 12. At a six percent interest rate, it will take you 12 years to double your money.

Investing

■ **Buy mutual funds.** This isn't very difficult, but you'll have to ask your parents to go with you to the brokerage when you open your account. Your parents can also open an account for you by computer on-line.

■ **Invest in stocks of companies** who make toys, games or other things you like. The prices of all the stocks are in the *Wall Street Journal.*

■ **Start a valuable collection.** If you are ten and start collecting things (stamps, coins, trading cards) now, by the time you're 21, your collection could be worth a small fortune.

■ **Save money for a trip.** You'll always end up with more than you need. (See "Saving Money" on page 5.)

BEARS AND BULLS

Here's what a couple of kids who sent us e-mail had to say about investing:

"Try the stock market. If you have enough money to invest some, you could make big $$. I once made over $1,000 on the stock market."

"I am the president of a stock market club. We get a membership card, track stocks, learn how to save a lot of money, get weekly newsletters, run businesses and with the money we make, we invest in the stocks we think are best!!!"

2.

Social Skills & Graces

Mind Your Manners

The whole idea of good manners is to make everybody feel comfortable by following the same set of rules. Here are some situations everybody has to deal with at one time or another.

Introductions

There are only a few rules for this, and they aren't very hard.

■ When introducing a kid to an older person, always mention the older person first. For example:

"Grandma, this is Hannah Sunshine. Hannah, this is my grandmother, Mrs. Traveller."

"Dad, this is Nick Johnson. Nick, this is my father, Mr. Strange."

Or, if your parents prefer to be called by their first names:

"This is my father, Howard."

You shouldn't call an adult by his or her first name unless you know it's okay with that person. Some grown-ups consider it really disrespectful.

■ When introducing a woman to a man, the woman's name should go first.

"Aunt Sue, this is my coach, Mr. Salineri. Coach, this is my aunt, Sue Smart."

■ When you are introduced, look at the person, smile, and say: "How do you do?" That's it. Unless you happen to think of something especially interesting, you don't have to say anything else.

■ The handshaking rule is this: boys and men shake hands with each other; boys and men shake hands with a woman or girl if she offers her hand first; if she doesn't, just smile and say, "How do you do?"

If you're introducing a woman to the President of the United States, the President's name goes first: *"Mr. President, this is my mother, Mrs. Strange."*

If the President offers your mother his hand, she will, of course, shake it. She should wait for him to offer it, though. Be sure to explain that to her if she should ever meet the President.

Royalty always goes first, too: *"Your Royal Highness, may I present my father, Mr. Strange?"*

It's a one-way street with presidents and royalty. People are presented to *them*—never the other way around.

Thanks

When do you have to write a thank-you note? When a gift is given or sent to you and the person is not there to be thanked personally. Get your thank-you notes out fast, or they'll just hang over your head and the person who gave you the gift might have hurt feelings or be annoyed.

Your letter can be short, but try to make it sincere and genuine.

> **Dear Aunt Martha,**
> **Thanks for the socks.**
> **Love,**
> **Charlie**

This isn't good enough. Add something that shows you put a little effort into it:

"Thanks for the socks. I really, really needed them because all my old ones have holes in them. And blue is my favorite color, too. I'll think of you every time I put them on."

And if you hated the socks, don't let your Aunt Martha know!

A Death

Even adults sometimes don't know quite what to do or say when someone dies. A boy whose best friend's father died unexpectedly had this good advice:

When my best friend's father died, my friend really didn't want to talk about it. All I could do was be with him as much as possible. I wanted him to know that I was always willing to talk, but I waited for him to bring the subject up. It took a long time. I used to think, "C'mon already—you should talk about it!" but he just wasn't ready.

Right after his father died, lots of kids called to say they were sorry. It was nice of them to call, but I could see it made him uncomfortable. Maybe it would have been easier if they had sent notes. I'm not sure.

My friend's father died a couple of years ago. Now sometimes I'll be the one to bring up his father. For example, "Did you do that with your Dad?" Right after his father died I waited for him to bring his father into the conversation.

I guess my best advice would be this: You should be ready to talk, but take your cues from the other person. Especially right after the death.

Phone Manners

Decent phone manners are simply a combination of common sense and courtesy. If you're making a call, always greet the person who answers the phone and always identify yourself.

"Hello, this is Dean. May I please speak to Andrew?"

Barking "Is Andrew there?" into the phone might get the job done, but you sure won't get points for politeness.

And if you're the one answering the phone, you've got to be polite, too.

Caller: *"Hello, is your father there?"*

You: *"No, I'm sorry, he's not. May I take a message?"*

When you take a message, always write it down, and repeat it back to the person to make sure you've got the name and phone number right.

Tying a Tie

Sometimes, if you have to go with your family to church or to visit people, you may have to wear a necktie. The easiest kind of necktie to wear is a clip-on, but a clip-on tie is for kids. Learn to tie your own necktie—something many grown-up men haven't figured out how to do! It's actually quite easy. The basic tie knot is called a *four-in-hand*. Practice in front of a mirror. The pictures are drawn as if you are looking in the mirror.

1. As you look in the mirror, the wide end of the tie should be on your right. The wide end should be about 6-8 inches longer than the narrow end, as it is in the picture.

2. Cross the wide end over the narrow end and then back underneath the narrow end.

3. Keep going around, and bring the wide end across the front of the narrow end again.

4. Now bring the wide end up the back through the neck loop.

5. Slip the wide end down through the loop at the front and tighten the knot.

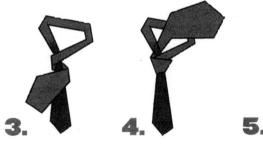

Voilà!

Tipping

I f you go to a restaurant or diner with your friends, remember to save enough money for a tip when you're deciding what to order.

A standard tip is about 15 percent of the bill. Don't be intimidated by the math! If you're lucky enough to live in an area where the tax is seven or eight percent, just double the tax. Here's another pretty easy way to rough out 15 percent.

First, figure out 10 percent, which is a snap: If your bill is $4.79, 10 percent is about 47 or 48 cents; 10 percent of $11.62 would be about $1.16. (You're moving over the decimal point one place to the left and dropping the last digit.) Once you have 10 percent, just divide that amount by 2 to get 5 percent. Add the two numbers together and you've got your 15 percent tip.

For example:

Your bill is $7.51. Ten percent is about 75 cents. Half of that is about 38 cents. Add those together to get $1.13 for a 15 percent tip. But it's easier to leave $1.15 so you don't have to count out pennies. Or $1.10. The tip doesn't have to be exactly 15 percent—just approximately that amount.

Of course, using a calculator is allowed—but every boy should know how to figure 15 percent!

Barbers and taxi drivers expect to be tipped, too.

WHERE DID TIPPING COME FROM, ANYWAY?

O ne theory goes that it started in the 1600s, when restaurants had boxes with *T.I.P.* written on them near their entrances. T.I.P. was short for "To Insure Promptness." Anyone who wanted to eat in a hurry would drop a few coins in the box before sitting down to eat.

THiNGS TO DO WHiLE YOU SiT iN A RESTAU-RANT WAiTiNG FOR THE FOOD TO COME

Coin Spinerino

Get a piece of paper or a napkin (or turn over the place mat if it's a paper one) and 3 draw circles to make a bull's-eye. Write *10* on the smallest circle, *5* on the medium-sized one and *1* on the biggest.

A heavy coin, like a quarter, is best for this spinning game. To start, put the quarter in the middle circle, hold it lightly in spinning position with one finger, and then spin it by snapping the quarter with the fingers of your other hand. You don't want the quarter to dance all over the table. Instead, you want a more controlled spin that will keep the coin in the target area.

When the coin stops spinning, you score the value of the circle it lands in. If it falls on a line, count the lower number. You can play against yourself by comparing the point value in, say, five or ten spins, and trying to better your score, or you can play against someone else at the table.

Snapping Straws

Flatten out two straws. Put the straws on top of each other and hold the two ends. Push you hands together, which will make the straws bend outward.

Now you're in snapping position. Quickly pull the straws out flat. If you're doing it right, the straws will make a loud snapping sound.

Friends

Friendship's most basic rule should be pretty familiar: *treat other people the way you want to be treated.* Be considerate of other people's feelings. Don't be a show-off, don't be mean or overly critical, don't lie, and if you do something wrong, learn to say "I'm sorry." If someone apologizes to you, accept the apology and try not to hold a grudge.

One kid says, "Always stick up for your friend. If he's done something wrong, tell him so in private, but not in front of other people."

HOW TO MAKE A FRIEND

Everyone feels a little shy when it comes to making new friends. There's always a chance that your show of friendship will be ignored, or rejected. Sometimes, though, you just have to take a chance.

Look around you and see if there's a kid who seems like he'd be fun to know. See how he treats his other friends. If he treats them well then chances are, he'd be a good friend to you, too.

Introduce yourself and ask the kid questions about himself, his family, and what he likes to do. Really listen to what he has to say. Look for things you have in common.

If he doesn't respond, remember that some kids who seem stuck-up are really just shy. Give him the benefit of the doubt. If he really is stuck-up, forget him and find someone better.

Sportsmanship

Take the good as well as the bad with a smile. Good sportsmanship goes beyond games—and into how you behave at school, at home, and with your friends.

It's not always easy to be a good sport, but try anyway. Don't sulk or whine if you lose. Don't make excuses like, "I hurt my leg," or "The sun got in my eyes." Don't blame your teammates or taunt your opponents.

A good sport is also a good winner—don't gloat! And, of course, never cheat.

How to Be a Real Jerk

Follow this simple advice and you're guaranteed to lose old friends and make new enemies:

1. Always make yourself the center of attention. Hog the spotlight and talk, talk, talk. If people aren't listening, just talk louder! *You're* the only one worth listening to, anyway.

2. Make sure everyone knows you're the most interesting kid around. If something exciting happened to someone else, be sure to tell people that the same thing happened to you, only better (or much, much worse). If Bobby says he's going to Disney World, tell him that's nothing: *you* got to go after closing time with a private party. Your uncle has connections.

3. Talk about your friends when they're not around. Don't say anything too bad—just let everyone know that Jim's dad went on the class trip because he lost his job. Or Tom's so very nice it kinda makes you wonder. . . . All you need to do is plant the seed. With luck, others will get credit for the rumor.

4. Make plans with your friend and if something better comes along, don't show up. (He doesn't mind—at least he's never said so.)

5. Make a habit of borrowing things from people—pencils, books, money, clothes, etc. Wait a few months before returning them—if you return them at all. *You'd* lend *your* stuff to them; they've just never asked.

6. Say whatever is on your mind, no matter how it makes people feel. You're just being honest, that's all. Besides, they shouldn't be so sensitive. If Paul's new haircut makes him look goofy, be sure to tell him so!

7. Always demand to get your own way. If Barry wants to play detective and you want to play horse, let the other kids know that Barry's idea is stupid, and so you won't have any part of it.

That's all it takes. Just follow these guidelines, and you'll soon get your number of friends down to the one or two who are too scared to tell you what they really think of you.

Party Stuff

How to Set a Table

The basic rule is knives and spoons on the right, forks on the left. The napkin can go on the plate, next to the fork, or under the fork. When you have more than one fork, you use them in order from left to right for each course. So if the salad will be served first, then place the salad fork on the far left. If fish is served next, then put that fork next, and so on. If you remember this rule, all the grown-ups at the table will watch you and follow your lead, because many of them have forgotten how to use fancy place settings.

If you're going to be *really* fancy and correct, bread plates go above the forks, water glasses above the knife and spoons.

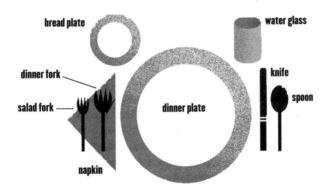

SETTING THE TABLE IN THE MIDDLE AGES

Ever heard the phrase, "He's a real trencherman"? Back in the Middle Ages people ate out of flat pieces of stale bread, called *trenchers*, instead of plates. The trenchers soaked up gravy and any uneaten bit of trencher was tossed to the dogs or given to the poor.

Forks were unknown in the Middle Ages. People carried around their personal spoons and knives, though. Two diners often shared a single trencher, bowl, or cup. Lots of people died from mysterious diseases.

Wrapping a Present—A Box or a Book

The trick to wrapping a rectangular present is to cut your paper to the right size. You should have enough to completely cover the present, but it shouldn't overlap too much on any side. Wrapping paper usually comes on a roll or in folded square sheets.

Using a Roll

Unroll some paper and place your present on it, lengthwise (a). Make sure you have enough paper for the width ends to overlap the sides of your present. Now you need to decide how much paper to cut from the roll.

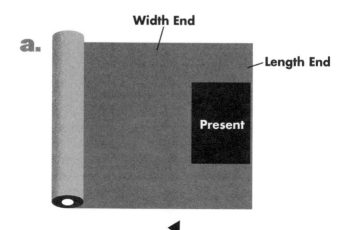

a.

Width End

Length End

Present

b.

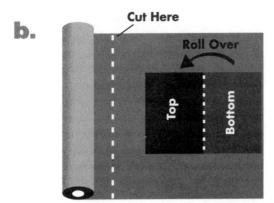

Align the long side of your present with the end of the roll and begin to slowly turn it over to its other side. Make allowances for both ends, plus a little extra for overlapping. Cut the paper from the roll (b). Now, put the present in the middle of the paper, upside-down. Bring the long sides together, and tape (c). Fold one of the ends into a V shape, and bring it over the sides, to the back of the present (d). Tape. Repeat on the other end.

c.   **d.**

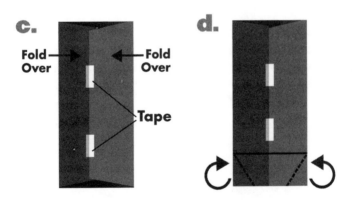

Using a Sheet

If you need to cut down a sheet of wrapping paper for your box, try to cut from just one end of the paper. Save the cut-off piece for later.

Oddly Shaped Presents

This is what tissue paper is for! Try to keep an assortment of brightly-colored tissue paper on hand. Put your present in the middle of several sheets of tissue. Gather the paper at the top of the bundle and tie on some curling ribbon. Curl ribbon with one edge of the scissors or a dull knife. For a younger person, decorate the package by tying a ribbon around the middle of a bag of M&Ms or Skittles and attaching it to the present. If your present has sharp edges that might tear the paper, you can first lay tissue on a piece of clear cellophane. Gather and tie.

Fast Homemade Piñata

If you have company coming for a party, but you don't have time to go to the store for a pinata, you can always make one yourself. You'll need:

- Lunch bags—one for each person
- Candy and small toys
- Old newspapers
- Four or more sturdy grocery bags
- String
- A wide (4") roll of masking tape
- Poster paint

Fill the lunch bags with the candy and toys. Twist the bags shut and write a kid's name on each bag. Put the lunch bags into one of the large grocery bags. Fill the rest of the bag with crumpled newspapers. Now, slip another grocery bag over the top of the first bag. Put both bags into a third bag and keep slipping one bag into another, until the piñata is too fat to go into one more bag. (The more layers you have, the stronger your piñata will be.)

Tie two strings around the piñata—one near the front and one near the back. Make sure you have enough string to hang the piñata. Start wrapping the tape around the piñata, and don't stop until it is completely covered. But don't cover up the ends of the string.

Paint the piñata and let it dry. Tie the ends of the string together, then tie another string through the loop. Hang the piñata from a tree or a hook.

To Make Your Piñata into an Animal

Make a piñata, as described. Draw or paint a paper plate to look like an animal's head. Tape or glue the plate to the "front" of the paper bag. Cut a piece of construction paper into quarters. Round the edges of each quarter to make a circle. Make a continuous coil out of each circle by cutting a spiral from the outside in.

Make some feet for your animal and glue them to one end of each coil. Then tape the four coil legs to the underside of the piñata. You can make a tail that way, too, or you can tie some yarn to the animal's tail end.

How to Shortsheet a Bed

Sometimes, a sleepover with friends can start to get boring. A good host never allows his guests to be bored. Here's how to liven things up at bedtime.

Method 1

Leave the bottom (fitted) sheet on the bed. Place the unhemmed end of the top sheet a third of the way down the bed, with the hemmed end facing the foot of the bed.

Fold the hemmed end over itself and bring it up towards the head of the bed to the place where the top sheet normally is (a). Tuck the sides of the top sheet in. Cover with blankets, a bedspread, or a quilt.

a.

Method 2:

Leave the bottom (fitted) sheet on the bed. Place the unhemmed end of the top sheet over the fitted sheet, leaving an extra two feet at the top (b).

Bring the hemmed end down towards the foot of the bed, then fold it over itself and bring it up to the place where it normally is. Tuck the top sheet in at the top and sides of the bed. Finish making the bed.

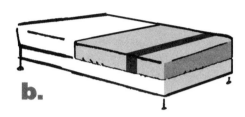

Scary Night Stuff

Here's a fun stunt to do for a Halloween party or sleepover. For the best effect, it needs to be done in a dark room. You'll need:

■ Two white sheets
■ Some cord
■ A directional lamp with a bright light bulb
■ A "patient"
■ Various easily identified objects (a screwdriver, a sponge, a rope, play food, an open can, etc.)

To set up your shadow operation

String the cord through the hem of the sheet and tie it to two vertical supports. This will be your screen. Put a bench or sturdy table directly behind the sheet, and cover it with another sheet—one that reaches the floor. Position the lamp so that its light shines on the bench, but not in the direction of the screen. Put all the objects to be removed from your "patient" in a cardboard box, behind the bench. One person will be the surgeon and another the patient. Have the patient lie on the bench with your audience on the other side of the screen.

Pick the moderator

He will tell the audience, "Ladies and gentlemen, today in our operating theater, we will attempt a dangerous operation. You see before you the surgeon. . . . Let's observe this highly skilled physician as he attempts to save the life of this long-suffering and mysteriously afflicted patient. . . ." Or something along those lines. The surgeon will pull various objects out from the box (patient's stomach) while the moderator continues his patter.

CREEPY BED THINGS

There's nothing worse than finding something in your bed that shouldn't be there.

Dead Hand

You will need:

■ A pair of surgical gloves
■ One box (four packages) of clear, unflavored gelatin
■ A rubberband

Make two packets of gelatin. Follow the directions on the package. Before it totally sets, pour the gelatin into one of the gloves. Do this over the sink. It helps to have someone hold the glove while you pour. There should be enough gelatin to fill two or three gloves. Don't fill the glove to the top. Tie off the top of the glove with the rubberband. Wrap the rubberband as tight as it will go. Rinse off the glove, and put it in the fridge to chill for a couple of hours.

When it's close to bedtime put the "dead hand" in your victim's bed, down near where you think his feet will be. Wait.

Snail Trails

"Once my friend put live snails on his sister's bed after she had fallen asleep. In the morning, there were trails of gooey stuff all over the bed. He never found the snails."

Homework

Making Excuses for Not Having Your Homework Done

1. My baby brother drooled all over it. (This actually works—a teacher said so.)

2. Guests came for dinner last night and my mom had to clean the house really fast. She put it somewhere, but she can't remember where.

3. There was a gas leak and we were evacuated for the night. We can't go back until they fix the leak.

4. My uncle won the lottery (in some other state). Everyone was so excited! I forgot all about my homework and my mom forgot to ask me.

5. We got last-minute tickets to see (check the paper for a game or show that night). I fell asleep in the car going home.

6. Our house was fumigated and we had to leave for the night. My homework's still in the house.

7. My (other) uncle came to our house unexpectedly. Actually, I just found out I have another uncle. You see, when my father was born, there was a twin, only the hospital told my grandparents that it had died. But actually the hospital had lost it, and they didn't want my grandparents to know. You see, there was a nurse there who wanted to have kids, but couldn't, and she stole it. She raised it as her own and nobody ever knew, until she died. By that time my uncle had grown up and moved away, but when his mother—not his real mother, but the nurse—died, she left a letter for him, telling him what she'd done. It kind of made sense to him, because he never had a birth certificate and he wasn't able to get one, because his mother (the nurse) told him she couldn't remember where he was born because of amnesia. Anyway, he and my father had a lot of catching up to do and everybody was pretty excited and crying and stuff. (This one's guaranteed to work. After all, who'd make it up?)

Advice

Some Good Advice

Always set goals. People who set goals for themselves get more done than people who don't. Make a list of what you want to do this day. At the end of the day, check off the goals you've met. If you didn't get to something, put it on tomorrow's list. Most people worry about the things they *didn't* do, without appreciating what they've done. By the end of the week you'll see that you accomplished a lot more than you think you did! Set long-term goals, too. Don't worry about whether they're practical or not, it's better to aim high.

Be curious. When someone asked Albert Einstein how he thought up the theory of relativity, he answered, "I just never stopped asking 'Why?'" Ask "Why?" "How?" "If?" and "What?"— then set about finding some answers. You won't find the answer to every question, but you'll learn a lot more than the person who doesn't ask or who thinks it's too much trouble.

Be brave. Being brave doesn't always mean being a war hero or running into a burning building to rescue a toddler. You're brave if you stand up for something you know is right, even when no one else seems to agree with you. If you know something's unfair, speak out. People will respect you for it, and more important, you'll respect yourself.

Follow through. Everyone starts a project with lots of enthusiasm, and that's important. But the test comes when a project stops being fun and starts to be just plain work. If you make yourself follow through the first time, you'll find that each time after, it gets easier and easier.

More Good Advice

Have a sense of humor. If you can laugh at yourself and your mistakes, you'll be more understanding of other people's mistakes. Use humor to try to keep your problems in perspective. Of course, there are some problems that are just too serious to laugh about, but most aren't.

Like yourself. There's a difference between laughing at yourself and putting yourself down. It makes people just as uncomfortable to hear you tearing yourself down as it does to hear you tearing down someone else. Take some time to appreciate the good things about yourself.

Be as honest as you can. Lies and half-truths have lives of their own. You may think you've gotten away with them, but they always return—and bring their friends! You should not only try to be straight with others, but be straight with yourself, too. If more than one person has said the same thing about you— especially if it's something you'd rather not hear—you may need to listen. There might be some truth in it.

Be flexible. If history has taught us one thing, it's that nothing ever stays the same. Don't become so attached to an idea that you become stuck. Keep yourself open to new ideas and experiences. It's important to know your own mind and to stand up for what you think is right, but if someone has a different opinion, hear them out politely. Even if you disagree, try to remember that other people's ideas have value, too.

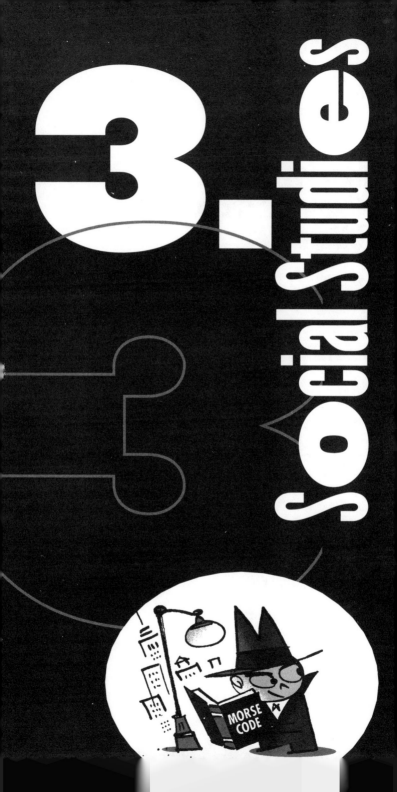

3. Social Studies

Every boy needs to know the basics of how the world around him works—politics, religion, family, and other stuff. . . .

How the Government Works

Checks and Balances

The Constitution distributes federal powers among three distinct branches of the government:

■ The Legislative branch (Congress), which makes the laws

■ The Executive branch (the President), which carries out the laws

■ The Judicial branch (the Supreme Court), which interprets the laws

To make sure too much power isn't concentrated in any one part of the government, the writers of the Constitution divided the power so that each of the three branches acts as a check on the other two. For example, the President is Commander-in-Chief of our military, but only Congress can declare war.

This constitutional system of checks and balances was designed to keep a single person or a small group from seizing power.

Congressional Facts

House of Representatives

The term of office for Representatives is two years. (The entire House is elected every two years.) To qualify as a representative, you have to be twenty-five years old, a U.S. citizen for seven years, and you have to live in the state from which you're elected.

■ All revenue bills (having to do with taxes and spending) are introduced from the House.

- The House has the power to *impeach,* or remove, civil officers.

- If no presidential candidate gets a majority of electoral votes, the House elects the President.

- The head of the House is called the *Speaker.*

Senate

Senators serve for six years. Like Representatives, they can be re-elected. To serve as a Senator you have to be at least thirty years old, a US citizen for nine years, and live in the state where you're elected.

- The Senate confirms all appointments made by the President.

- It approves treaties and tries anyone who's impeached.

- The Vice President presides over the Senate.

- If no vice-presidential candidate gets a majority of electoral votes, the Senate elects the Vice President.

Presidential Facts

The term of office for the President is four years. A President can be re-elected once. To qualify for President, you have to be thirty-five years old, a native-born citizen, and a resident of the United States for fourteen years.

- The President is Commander-in-Chief of the armed forces.

- The President negotiates treaties with foreign governments, appoints federal officials, can pardon any offense against the federal government except impeachment, and can *veto* (say "no" to) bills passed by Congress.

Impeachment

If the President or any other high government official breaks the law, the Constitution offers a way to help solve the problem: Article II, Section 4 of the Constitution provides that the President can be removed from office by the process of impeachment if accused of treason, bribery, or other "high crimes and misdemeanors." The House has the power to impeach. If the President is impeached, the next step is a trial before the Senate. When that happens, the Chief Justice of the Supreme Court acts as the presiding officer—not the Vice President. So far, no President has ever been removed from office by impeachment.

HOW TO WRITE TO YOUR REPRESENTATIVE AND SENATORS

First, find out your Representative or Senator's name. If you aren't sure, look in a newspaper or ask your parents or teachers, or go to the library.

Address your envelope like this:

> Senator (senator's name)
> United States Senate
> Washington, DC 20510

> Representative (representative's name)
> United States House of Representatives
> Washington, DC 20510

In your letter, start off by using this fancy form of address at the top of the page:

> The Honorable (name)
> United States House of Representatives
> (or United States Senate)
> Dear Representative/Senator (name):

Then write your letter. Be sure to include your name and address after your signature so your legislator can respond to you.

Facts about the Supreme Court

No qualifications for membership in the Supreme Court are stated in the Constitution. You don't even have to be a lawyer to be a Supreme Court Justice.

The Court consists of one Chief Justice and eight Associate Justices. Each member of the court is appointed by the President and must be approved by the Senate. Supreme Court appointments are for life, unless a Justice is impeached. But Justices can retire if they wish.

The Supreme Court hears cases in which a state or the federal government is involved; cases dealing with ambassadors or other foreign ministers; and cases appealed from lower courts, especially if there's a Constitutional question.

THE ORDER OF SUCCESSION TO THE PRESIDENCY

These are the people, in order, who take over if the president dies or leaves office for some reason.

1. The Vice President
2. Speaker of the House
3. President *pro-tempore* of the Senate
4. Secretary of State
5. Secretary of the Treasury
6. Secretary of Defense
7. Attorney General
8. Postmaster General
9. Secretary of the Interior
10. Secretary of Agriculture
11. Secretary of Commerce
12. Secretary of Labor

Democrats and Republicans

These two major US political parties can trace their roots back to the early days of our country. There are many other, smaller parties in the US, including the Libertarian Party, the Green Party and the Reform Party.

Democratic Party

The Democratic party is the oldest political party in the country. It developed from the Anti-Federalist party led by Thomas Jefferson. This Anti-Federalist party first called itself the "Republicans." After the Federalist party died out, the Republicans were the only party, but they soon split into two wings, the Democratic Republicans and the National Republicans. Under the leadership of Andrew Jackson, the Democratic Republicans became known simply as "Democrats," the name they've kept ever since.

As a rule, Democrats look to government for help solving problems in society.

THE FLAG

Each part of the American flag is symbolic. Traditionally, the red on the flag stands for courage, white for liberty, and blue for loyalty. The 13 stripes represent the 13 original colonies. Each star represents one state.

Republican Party

Although it didn't come into true existence until much later, the Republican party traces its origin back to Alexander Hamilton's Federalist party. When the Federalist party fizzled out, the opponents of the Democratic Republicans (Jefferson's party that went on to become the "Democrats") called themselves National Republicans.

This group went on to become the Whig party, which opposed Andrew Jackson's Democrats. In 1854, the Whig party splintered over the issue of slavery. Out of this division a new, third, party was formed: the Republicans. Abraham Lincoln was the first Republican President.

As a rule, Republicans look to individuals to help solve problems in society.

THE AMERICAN EAGLE

Benjamin Franklin wanted the wild turkey to be our national bird, but he didn't get his wish. Congress chose the American Bald Eagle as our national bird in 1782.

The eagle is now protected by law. It is illegal for anyone except for members of certain Indian tribes to have or collect eagle feathers. The name "bald eagle" comes from how the white feathers look on the bird's head—not because it's bald.

You can find the Bald Eagle on the National Seal, coins, military badges, and other government objects.

Families

The primary political unit in every society is the family. The more stable and secure families are, the better and healthier society is.

A Family Experiment

Every family has a set of rules—the way things work—even if its members don't know it. Try writing down the "rules" for your family and sharing them at the family dinner table. You'll be surprised at how many family members you surprise!

Parents

Parents are human. They can't always keep their problems to themselves. Still, it's not fair for them to involve you in their fights and it's especially not fair for them to make you choose sides. If one (or both) of your parents is doing this, point out to them that their fighting upsets you. Suggest that they talk over their differences when you're not around or that they take a nice long walk, to work things out. Point out that you love them both and you only like taking sides when watching your favorite team.

Too-strict parents. You might be surprised to learn that most kids would rather have parents that are a little too strict than not strict enough. When they make rules about your behavior— even if they seem overly strict—your parents are showing you they really care about the things you do, and who you do them with. Learning about life is a little like learning to fly an airplane. Once you get in the air it's exciting, but first you need to know which buttons to press and which ones to leave alone. If your flight instructor puts you in a plane and says, "Figure out the rules yourself. Good luck!" you know you're in trouble. It's the same with parents.

You need to earn your parents' trust. If you can do this now when you're young, they'll trust you later with bigger things. In other words, if they can't count on you now to bring in your bike at night, you're going to have trouble getting the keys to the family car later on.

Siblings

It may be asking too much to be best friends with your brother or sister, but you can make things go smoother if you have a few ground rules. Here's how some kids have dealt with the fighting-between-siblings issue.

■ Be the bigger of the two, and ignore what he or she just did or said. This is hard!

■ Stop yourself before you hit or yell. Talk it out.

■ Stop yourself before bringing your parents into it. Can it be worked out between the two of you? Chances are, your parents will still be looking for a solution long after you and your sibling have forgotten all about the problem.

■ If you must have it out, make some fair fighting rules, like:

1. No hitting (or kicking or spitting).

2. No yelling.

3. No name calling.

4. No accusing.

Other Relatives

Aunt: Your mother or father's sister, or your uncle's wife.

Uncle: Your mother or father's brother, or your aunt's husband.

Cousin: Your aunt and uncle's child.

First cousin, once removed: Your mother or father's cousin.

Second cousin: Your parent's cousin's child.

Great-aunt or great-uncle: Your grandparent's sibling. (Genealogists call this relationship grand-aunt or -uncle.) A great-aunt is (for instance) your great-grandmother's sister.

Half-sibling: Your mother or father's child with a previous spouse.

Step-sibling: Your mother's husband's (or father's wife's) child from a previous marriage.

Divorce

In the past 50 years, many more marriages than ever before are coming apart. Today, more than half of all marriages fail. This is one of society's biggest problems. Whether it's your own parents who are divorcing, or a good friend's parents, this is never easy on kids. Even knowing that lots of other kids are going through, or have gone through, the same thing doesn't make it easier. Just remember: it isn't your fault. Try to do better when it's your turn.

If it's your parents who are breaking up, remember that your mother and father are divorcing each other—they're not divorcing you or your brothers and sisters. Try not to take sides, even if you're tempted. If your parents complain about each other to you, ask them not to. As a matter of fact, even if your parents aren't divorced, don't let them get away with this kind of thing—it puts a kid in a terrible position.

Sometimes it's very hard to tell your friends that your parents are breaking up. Try to do it, though, so you won't feel as though you're carrying a horrible secret around. It's almost always better to talk things out.

Occasionally you'll already know that a good friend's parents are separating, but your friend might be having a hard time telling you. If that happens, after a couple of weeks bring it up yourself, but in a natural, sympathetic way. You might say, for example, "I'm sorry about your parents." You don't have to say too much; just let your friend know you're aware of the situation, and that you're still his friend.

If you or a friend need to cry, don't be embarrassed.

Religion

Here are the five largest religions in the world; we've listed them here beginning with the oldest.

Hinduism

This is the oldest of all the major religions and the largest religion in India. Hindus believe that after death they are reborn (reincarnated) into different bodies. They believe that if they live decent lives, their *karma* will be good and they will be reincarnated as prosperous or spiritual people. On the other hand, if they are wicked, they might come back as beggars—or even animals. Hindus worship many individual gods, like Siva, Ganesh, and Hanuman, but believe that all these gods are just different parts of the one great power—Brahman. To show their respect for the gods, Hindus bathe every day and offer the gods food and incense on small altars in their homes. The *Bhagavad-Gita* is a Hindu book of scripture.

Judaism

Jews believe that nearly 6,000 years ago, one god, Yaweh, revealed his laws to the people of Israel through a prophet named Moses. Before Judaism, the people of Israel had believed in many gods. The most sacred writings in Judaism are the *Bible* (the part Christians refer to as the *Old Testament*) and the *Talmud*—commentaries on the *Bible* written by holy men called *rabbis*. The *Bible* contains a "history" of humankind and of the Jewish people beginning with Abraham, who is considered to be the first Jew. It also contains God's revelations to the many Jewish prophets who followed Abraham. Each Jewish temple (called a *synagogue*) keeps a scroll (the *Torah*) with the laws of God written on it. Jews believe that God will someday send a *messiah*, a holy messenger, to solve all the problems of the world. Jewish holidays include Passover (which celebrates the Jews' safe passage out of slavery in Egypt) and Rosh Hashanah. Jewish children enjoy celebrating Hanukkah and Purim. When they are thirteen years old, Jewish boys and girls have a bar- or bat-mitzvah. For this coming-of-age ceremony, they must memorize and recite passages from the *Bible*.

Buddhism

Gautama Buddha was a wealthy prince who lived in Northern India over 2,500 years ago. He gave up his position and riches in order to seek knowledge or *enlightenment.* One day as he sat thinking under a banyan tree, he was suddenly filled with all the knowledge of the world. He understood that humankind could become free of the cycle of birth, death, and rebirth only if we treated our enemies with kindness, and stopped looking for happiness in worldly things. Any person able to do this would achieve *nirvana, or* eternal happiness. Buddhists hope to attain enlightenment and reach nirvana by practicing a deep kind of thought—called meditation—and by following the example provided by Gautama, the Buddha. From India, Buddhism has spread to China, Tibet, Japan, Southeast Asia, and elsewhere.

Christianity

Two thousand years ago, a Jew named Jesus was born in Bethlehem, Israel. Before his birth, prophets had predicted the coming of a Jewish messenger from God. Some Jews believed that this baby was the Messiah, or Christ. As a young man, Jesus proclaimed himself to be the promised Messiah and began teaching throughout the land. He began to attract followers, and amazed them by performing miracles, such as healing the sick, walking on water, and raising the dead. Jesus explained that he would sacrifice his life on Earth so those who believed in him would have eternal life in heaven. Soon the rulers of the land decided that Jesus was a threat to their power and so they put him to death. Three days after his death, it was reported that Jesus's body had risen, resurrected from death, and later he was seen visiting some of his followers. In these visitations, Jesus promised eternal life to anyone who would follow his example. Like Buddha, Jesus Christ taught forgiveness and compassion. He urged people to put their faith in godly, rather than worldly, things. The Christian *Bible* includes not only the Old Testament, but also the New Testament, which records Jesus Christ's life and death. Major Christian holidays are Christmas—which celebrates Christ's birth—and Easter, the holiest day in the Christian calendar, which celebrates Jesus's resurrection.

Islam

Like Christianity, Islam also has its roots in Judaism. It is the most recent of all the major religions, and the fastest-growing. Muslims believe that the Messiah came to Earth 1,300 years ago and that his name is Mohammed. The prophet Mohammed showed people how God (Allah) wished them to live and worship. God's word is written down in a holy book, called the *Koran*. All devout Muslims pray five times a day, no matter where they are. When they pray (on special rugs which they carry with them), they always face the holy city of Mecca, in Saudi Arabia. Once a year, all Muslims show their respect for God by fasting during the holiday called *Ramadan*. Ramadan lasts for one month, and during that time, Muslims are not allowed to eat or drink during daylight hours. Fasting reminds all Muslims that their bodies are less important than their souls in the eyes of God. At the end of Ramadan, there is a great feast. All Muslims are expected to make a pilgrimage to Mecca at least once during their lifetimes.

All five of the world's major religions teach respect towards others, both in thought and deed. In all five religions, failure to obey religious laws has very serious consequences. For some, this means a cycle of birth and rebirth in a series of lifetimes, while for others the punishment is separation from God in this life or after death.

What Other Kids Like

We asked a lot of kids what kinds of books they liked and which movies they liked. We also asked parents what they thought. Here are some of our "poll" results:

A Random List of Things Kids Say Other Kids Should Know by the Time They're 12

■ How to introduce themselves to strangers

■ How to navigate in their hometown, buy stuff at a store, and return home

■ Have a library card and know how to use the library

■ How to say simple words in one foreign language

■ How to order at a restaurant

■ Basic mastery of geography: the four oceans, seven continents, etc.

■ How to feed themselves (prepare a meal, make a snack)

■ How to relate to the opposite sex in an appropriate way

■ Basic telephone etiquette

■ How to do homework without parental prodding or oversight

- Basic mastery of one musical instrument (drums not included)
- How to ride a bike
- How to swim
- Be skilled in at least one sport
- Roger Maris hit 61 home runs in '61
- Basic things about the human reproductive system
- The approximate dates of:
    - The American Revolution
    - The Civil War
    - World War I
    - The Great Depression
    - World War II
    - The Civil Rights movement

Movies

Most of these have stood the test of time!
- *Wizard of Oz*
- *Around the World in 80 Days*
- *Lady and the Tramp*
- *The Court Jester*
- *Hans Christian Andersen*
- *The Thief of Baghdad*
- *A Night at the Opera*
- *Seven Brides for Seven Brothers*
- *On the Town*
- *Damn Yankees*
- *Robin Hood* (the Errol Flynn version, of course!)
- *Fort Apache*
- *Casablanca*

A List of Great Books for Kids

If you haven't read the books on this list yet, you're in for a real treat!

- *The Wind in the Willows* by Kenneth Grahame
- Any of the seven books in *The Chronicles of Narnia* by C. S. Lewis
- *Charlotte's Web* and *Stuart Little* by E. B. White
- *A Wrinkle in Time* by Madeleine L'Engle
- Anything by Roald Dahl
- *The Oxford Book of Poetry for Children* compiled by Edward Blishen and illustrated by Brian Wildsmith
- *Bible* stories
- *Stories for Children* by Isaac Bashevis Singer

A Reading Club

Start a "literary society" in your neighborhood with other kids. This is a great way to share ideas about the things you've read—and find out about new books and authors you might like.

Here's how it works. Hold a meeting and elect a *convenor*. The convenor is the person who runs the meetings of the society. At the first meeting, decide which book everyone should read. Then every week, meet and discuss the book together as you read it. The whole club should focus on the same book at the same time and all the activities should be related to the book.

Top Five Board Games:

- Risk
- Stratego
- Monopoly
- Clue
- Chess

Kid Bonus: 13 Dead-End Drive

THE BEST BOYS' BOOKS

Mr. Popper's Penguins by Richard and Florence Atwater

The Freddy the Pig stories by Walter Brooks

Just So Stories by Kipling

Treasure Island by R.L. Stevenson

Tom Sawyer by Mark Twain

Penrod by Booth Tarkington

Boy and *Going Solo* by Roald Dahl

The *Tintin* series by Herge

Peter Pan by J. M. Barrie (This was originally a play, but there are several prose versions available.)

For example, let's say you choose *Treasure Island* by Robert Louis Stevenson. One week, you might have a treasure hunt using a pirate's map. Another week, you might play pirates in the playground and try to take over each other's ship. If the meeting is on a rainy day, you might hold it at the library and look at pictures of different kinds of pirate ships. Or you might check out a copy of the movie "Treasure Island," starring Robert Newton. If you can talk like Robert Newton does in the movie, you'll be able to talk like a real pirate. Har! Once you're all done with *Treasure Island,* you can start on a new story—maybe *Peter Pan,* where you can meet the magnificently terrifying Captain Hook!

TOP FIVE CARD GAMES:

- Poker
- Casino
- Hearts
- Gin
- War

4.

Safety, Hygiene & Grooming

You never know when an emergency will occur—that's why they call them "emergencies." Here's what you can do to be prepared:

Safety First

Fire

- If you have a clear path, get out of the building right away and don't go back in for ANYTHING.
- Call the fire department from a neighbor's house.
- If you are on fire: STOP, DROP, and ROLL.
- If you're in a smoke-filled room, get down on the floor. Smoke rises. If you can, place a wet towel over your nose and breathe through it.
- If there's a fire in the next room, close all adjoining doors. NEVER OPEN THE DOORS if you suspect a fire in the next room. Touch the door carefully to see if it's warm. If it is, jam wet towels or pillow cases in the space between the door and the floor. Don't open any windows until the door is well sealed. (An open window can create a draft, attracting the fire.) If you can, turn on the shower and get in it.
- If you're in a tall building, tie something white to a stick and wave it out the window, so fire fighters can find you.
- If there isn't any water or a fire extinguisher around, you can put out a small fire with sand or dirt. (For example, grab a potted plant and dump the dirt on the flames.)

Thunderstorms

In a thunderstorm, lightning is drawn to tall objects, like trees and buildings. Though you'll want to find shelter under a tree, make sure it's not the tallest one around. Also, don't stand on a tree's roots or touch its trunk during a thunderstorm. When struck by lightning, the electrical charge runs through a tree—from the tips of each branch to the ends of each root. It will also travel through the ground surrounding the tree.

All tall buildings are equipped with lightning rods (a metal rod that runs from the roof to the ground, attracting and absorbing any electrical charge) so you're safe even in a very tall building. Golfers are sometimes hit by lightning because they stand out on the fairway. If you're on a beach or golf course (or any other flat, featureless area), lie down flat on the ground, until the storm passes. But stay away from the water. You're usually safe in your car, because the rubber in a car's tires doesn't conduct electricity.

"Rotten Eggs"

Luckily, most people in life are good. But there are some "rotten eggs"out there. The problem is, you can't usually tell who's a rotten egg and who isn't. They don't wear signs. That's why it's important to trust your instincts and use some common sense. If a stranger (or even someone you know) is acting overly friendly or offering you stuff, be on your guard. (Be especially cautious if the person wants to take you somewhere where there aren't other people around.) It's not normal for a grown-up to want to be your best friend. If someone's acting like they want to be a "special" friend, let them know that you already have a best friend—someone your own age. Get away from strangers who make you uncomfortable as quickly as possible.

TICK REMOVAL

These three proven tick-removal methods work on both people and pets. Use them to remove regular ticks (not the tiny ones that carry Lyme disease. If you think you have one of these, call your vet or doctor for advice).

Method One: Cover the tick with petroleum jelly. Wait a few minutes for the tick to back out. Grab it and flush it down the toilet. If this doesn't work, try method two.

Method Two: Place several drops of turpentine or kerosene on the tick. When it backs out, remove and destroy. If neither of these work, you'll have to resort to method three (it's gross but it always works).

Method Three. Place the prongs of a pair of tweezers on either side of the tick's body. Carefully rotate the tweezers as you pull up (like unscrewing a bottle top). Gently pull until the whole tick pops out. Destroy. If you aren't careful, you may just remove the tick's body, while leaving the head embedded. If this happens, dab alcohol on the spot where the head is. Continue dabbing until the tick falls out.

It's not necessary to run to the doctor every time you get a tick bite, but make sure you always wash the bitten area thoroughly with soap and water after removing one.

Skin Deep

There's a saying that beauty is only skin-deep. That's not true, of course, since many hearts are beautiful and so are all souls. But it is a good reminder to keep the part of us that everybody can see nice and clean.

There are three basic hygiene rules you need to know to survive socially:

1. Take a shower. If you play sports, you need to do this every day.

2. Use deodorant. You probably won't need to do this until you reach puberty, but you'll know when you need it.

3. Brush your teeth. Your dentist would probably tell you to brush after every meal, but if you can't, twice a day should suffice—just make sure one of those times is before you leave the house for the first time each day.

A QUICK NOTE ABOUT ZITS

They happen to just about everyone, including many adults, so don't panic. Use a medicated acne cream (available in drugstores), wash your face regularly, and try not to pick at them. If they get really bad, ask a parent to take you to a dermatologist.

5.

Stuff to Eat

Lots of people sent us a whole bunch of things you can do with food. Some of these snacks have to be cooked first—and that means *heat.* And heat means burns, if you aren't careful. Anything involving a stove can be dangerous, so make sure your parents know what you're doing. If you aren't sure what you're doing, get an adult to give you a hand. That way, you'll live to be an adult someday yourself.

Snacks

Cinnamon Toast

You will need:

- A medium-size jar with lid
- 1 cup sugar
- 2 tablespoons cinnamon
- 2 slices of bread (per person)
- Butter or margarine

Measure the sugar and cinnamon into the jar, put on the lid, and shake until mixed.

Spread the butter on toasted bread and, when it melts, sprinkle one teaspoon of cinnamon-sugar on top of each slice. Make cinnamon-sugar up ahead of time, and always keep a jar of it handy.

comes from the inner bark of a tree that grows on the
island of Sri Lanka. It was one of the precious spices that
Columbus was seeking when he accidentally bumped into
North America.

Popovers

You will need:

- A muffin pan (the heavier the better)
- Butter for greasing muffin pan
- A flour sifter
- A hand mixer or whisk
- 1½ cups of flour
- ½ teaspoon salt
- 3 eggs
- 1½ cups milk
- 2 tablespoons melted butter

It's the steam inside them that makes popovers "pop." The
secret is to have an oven that's not too hot (they'll brown
before they pop) or too cold (they'll flop, not pop). So—after
you've gotten all your ingredients together and greased your
muffin tins, heat your oven to 450°, then:

Sift the flour and salt into a mixing bowl. In another bowl (or a
large measuring cup) beat the eggs, milk, and melted butter
together. Slowly, add the liquid to the dry ingredients, mixing with
a hand mixer or a whisk all the while. Continue mixing for two
minutes, or until the batter has no lumps and is the consistency
of melted ice cream. Pour the batter into the well-greased muffin pan. Fill them up a little past halfway (the batter will rise a lot)
and put the pan in the middle of the oven. Leave it there for fif-
teen minutes, then reduce the temperature to 350° and continue
baking them another 20 minutes. *Do not open the oven door,* or
your popovers will be flopovers. Take them out and serve immediately. If you want to get fancy, mix together some softened,
whipped butter with your favorite jam and spread in the steam-
ing popovers. Makes 12.

Real Food

Weineritos

For each person, you will need:

- One corn tortilla
- One hot dog
- One slice of American cheese
- Catsup

In the microwave: Soften the tortilla first, by putting it on a microwave-safe plate with a dampened paper towel on top. Cook for 30 seconds. Take the tortilla out of the oven. Put on the tortilla: a piece of American cheese, a hot dog, and a little catsup. Now roll up the tortilla and put it, seam side down, on the plate. Cover with the paper towel and "nuke" for an additional 45 seconds. If you are cooking more than one at a time, cook them for one minute.

A BRIEF HISTORY OF THE HOT DOG

It all started over 3,000 years ago with the Babylonians, who came up with the idea of stuffing meat into animal intestines—the first sausages. The Greeks and Romans loved sausages, too. As a matter of fact, the oldest known Roman cookbook mentions sausages.

A German city, Frankfurt, had its own version of the sausage, which became known as the "frankfurter."

Another nickname for frankfurters was "dachshund" sausages—named for the little, long German dogs they resemble. The story goes that in 1906 a cartoonist named Tad Dorgan was watching a baseball game and heard a vendor shouting, "Get your red hot Dachshund dogs!" He thought a picture of a real dachshund in a bun, covered with mustard, would make a good cartoon. He sketched it, but wasn't sure how to spell "dachshund," so settled for "hot dog." The rest is history.

Quesadillas

You will need:

- 2 flour tortillas
- A handful of grated Monterey Jack or cheddar cheese
- A pastry brush

In the microwave: Place the flour tortilla on a microwave-safe plate and put a handful of Jack or cheddar cheese in the middle of it. Brush water around the edges of the tortilla, and put another tortilla on top to make the quesadillas. Press down on the quesadilla, flattening the cheese and pressing out any trapped air as you do. The water will "glue" the two tortillas together. Cover the quesadilla with a damp paper towel, and nuke for one minute.

Remove from oven and cut into wedges, like a pizza. Serves 2.

Some variations for the adventurous: Add refried beans; shredded, cooked chicken or beef; sweet or mild chile peppers; olives, etc.

WHAT IS "MONTEREY JACK"?

The Jacks were a large land-owning family in the town of Monterey, California. They produced a mild, white cheese at their ranch, which came to be known as "Jack's cheese," and eventually "Monterey Jack."

Basic Pizza

You will need:

- 1 package of fast-rising dry yeast
- 2½ cups of flour
- 2 teaspoons of salt
- A spoonful of sugar
- 1 cup of hot tap water
- 1 small can of tomato paste
- 8 ounces of shredded mozzarella cheese
- Some vegetable oil (olive oil is best)

The Crust

- First, wash your hands. Put the entire package of yeast and a spoonful of sugar in a large mixing bowl. Add one cup of hot-but-not-scalding water and stir just enough to mix the yeast evenly in the water. When the mixture begins to bubble (this is the live yeast growing) add one cup of the flour and stir with a sturdy spoon. Gradually, add one more cup of the flour, until the mixture is too thick to stir.

- Pour a little oil onto your hands and rub them together. Gently begin to punch the dough in the bowl, first with one fist, and then with the other. When the dough begins to stick to your hands, add the remaining ½ cup of flour a little at a time. When the pizza dough feels springy under your hands—usually after 5 minutes of kneading—cover the bowl with a damp towel. Put the bowl in a warm place for about 45 minutes, or until the dough is twice its original size.

- While the dough is rising, preheat the oven to 500° and oil a round pizza pan or a cookie sheet. This is a good time to grate the cheese, if you didn't buy it pre-shredded.

- Check to see if the dough has finished rising by poking your finger into the middle of it. If the dent stays, it's time to move the pizza dough out of the bowl (it will collapse a little) and into the pan. Gently push and stretch the dough until it covers the pan. Fold over the outside edges of the dough to make a raised crust.

The Topping

■ Scoop out some tomato paste with a spoon or your fingers and spread it on the dough. Spread it right up to the edges. You don't need much—just enough for a thin, red layer. If you put on too much sauce, or it's too watery, the bottom of the crust won't cook through. Sprinkle the grated cheese evenly over the pizza.

■ Put the pizza on the lowest rack of your oven, and turn the oven down to 450°. After ten minutes, check to see how your pizza is doing. If the cheese is melted—but not burned—and the crust is a golden brown, it's ready. If not, leave it in for another five minutes.

Really Fast Pizza

If making pizza from scratch seems too complicated (it's not!), you can always use frozen or refrigerated dough. Or, you can substitute:

■ A loaf of French bread, sliced lengthwise

■ English muffin halves

■ Flour tortillas or pita bread halves, for a really thin crust

■ Biscuit dough

Prepare as for the Basic Cheese Pizza.

A Complete Stick-to-Your-Ribs Supper: Meatloaf & Mashed Potatoes

You will need:

■ 2 pounds of ground meat: beef, pork, veal, turkey, or chicken (or any combination)

■ ¾ cup of bread crumbs

■ 1 egg

■ ½ cup chopped onion

■ Catsup

■ 4 large Idaho potatoes

■ 4 ounces (half a stick) of butter

■ 1 cup milk

- Salt and pepper
- A loaf or deep-sided baking pan
- A mixing bowl
- A potato masher or sturdy fork
- Vegetable of your choice (fresh, frozen, or canned)

Before you start:

- Wash your hands!
- Heat oven to 400°.
- Take out the butter and milk and let sit until it's time to mash the potatoes.

Meatloaf
- In a large mixing bowl, combine meat, bread crumbs, egg, onion, salt, and pepper. Using your hands, mix the ingredients together, until the egg and bread crumbs are evenly distributed in the meat. Put the meatloaf in a bread pan or mound it into a baking dish with high sides. Spread a layer of catsup on top and place the meatloaf in the middle of your oven.

Potatoes
- Wash the potatoes. Prick a few holes in them with a fork and put them in the oven with the meatloaf. Cook the meat and potatoes for 50 minutes, then check the potatoes by sticking a fork in them. If it slides in easily, they're done. Turn the oven off and take out the potatoes, leaving the meatloaf in the oven.

FYi

1 quart = 4 cups
1 pint = 2 cups
1 cup = 8 fluid ounces
1 cup = 16 tablespoons
1/3 cup = 5 tablespoons plus 1 teaspoon
1 fluid ounce = 2 tablespoons
3 teaspoons = 1 tablespoon

- Cut the potatoes in half, lengthwise. Place a potato half— flat side down—on a dinner plate, and pinch the skin together. The jacket will slide off, leaving the insides exposed. (Do this carefully, they're HOT!) Pick out any dark bits and put the potatoes in a bowl. Continue, until all of the skins have been removed. (If you *like* potato skins, put the jackets back in the oven, and let them crisp for a few minutes.) Add the milk, butter, salt and pepper to the potatoes and mash them with a fork or a potato masher.

- When you've finished mashing the potatoes, take the meatloaf out of the oven and drain off any extra fat. Move it to a serving plate, and slice. Serve with the mashed potatoes and a vegetable. Serves 4.

Treats

Fried Worms

You will need:

- Graham cracker crumbs
- Tootsie Rolls

Put the graham cracker crumbs in a bag.

With wrapper off, roll the Tootsie Roll back and forth in your hands, like clay. When the Tootsie Roll is long and soft and wormy, put it in the bag of graham crackers. Shake and serve on a lettuce leaf.

Peanut Butter and Frosting Sandwiches

This is one kid's favorite after-school snack and a good way to use up extra frosting.

- Spread peanut butter on one slice of bread.
- Spread chocolate frosting on the other slice.
- Put the two slices together.

Kick-Me-Til-I-Scream

It's a recipe, it's a game . . . it's just fun!

You'll need two empty coffee cans—a one-pounder and a two-pounder, plus the plastic lids that come with them. Fill the smaller can almost to the top with ice cream custard. (The recipe comes next.) Put the plastic lid on, and tape the top really, really well. Packing tape works best.

Next, put the smaller can in the bigger can and layer crushed ice (see "How to Crush Ice," below) and rock salt all around it until it reaches the top.

Now put the plastic lid on the bigger can and make sure it's taped together really well. Don't be stingy with the tape—the more the better.

Take the can outside and kick it around for about 20 minutes. Unwrap the can and grab a spoon—you've just made ice cream.

Peppermint-Stick Ice Cream Custard

You will need:

- ¼ lb. peppermint-stick candy
- 1 cup milk
- ½ cup cream
- ½ cup whipping cream
- 1 tray of ice cubes

How To Crush Ice

Put one trayful of ice cubes in a large, square piece of clean cloth—a large handkerchief is perfect. Twist the top, so the ice won't come out, and hit the cloth with the side of a hammer or an iron skillet. Make sure you do this on something hard, like a cement patio, NOT on a tile floor or a rug.

Grind up or crush ¼ lb. of peppermint-stick candy (about nine sticks). Soak the candy in one cup of milk. The longer you soak it, the mintier the ice cream will taste. Add ½ cup cream and ½ cup whipping cream.

Root Beer Float

Put a scoop of vanilla ice cream in a tall glass. Pour root beer over the ice cream, until it fizzes to the top of the glass. In some parts of the country, this is called a Black Cow.

Milk Shake or Malted

For a chocolate shake: Put one or two scoops of softened vanilla ice cream in a tall glass. Pour some chocolate syrup on the ice cream, then add a little milk. Stir with an electric hand mixer or with a fork, breaking up the ice cream, as you do. Continue stirring, until it's completely mixed. For a malted, add a tablespoon of malted milk powder.

For a vanilla shake: Instead of chocolate syrup, use a tea-spoonful of vanilla.

Chocolate-Covered Frozen Bananas

You will need:
- 6 bananas
- A small (6-ounce) bag of chocolate chips, melted
- Popsicle sticks
- A small cookie sheet
- A spatula

Peel the bananas, then cut them in half crosswise. Place a Popsicle stick in the end of each half. Lay the bananas on a cookie sheet and freeze them for several hours, until they are frozen solid. Melt the chocolate chips in a microwave or double boiler. With the spatula, spread melted chocolate on the frozen bananas. The chocolate should harden instantly. Wrap any uneaten bananas in aluminum foil and store them in the freezer.

LUNCHROOM CONVERSATION STOPPERS

The next time someone complains about the cafeteria food, tell them it could be worse:

In China they could be feasting on roasted water beetles, steamed cat, or hundred-year-old eggs (eggs that have been pickled in brine, coated with a paste of clay and ashes and buried in the ground for several months—not years, as the name implies.) Earthworms, caterpillars, grasshoppers, and flies also find their way into the Chinese wok. In Zanzibar, termite and banana pie is a favorite dessert. Ghana boasts stewed rat, while in France they prefer theirs marinated in wine, brushed with olive oil, and grilled over a fire of broken wine barrels.

Cruella DeVil is not the only one who has designs on one of our favorite pets, the dog. In Myanmar, it is served boiled and stuffed, while Indonesians marinate their dog du jour in coconut cream and serve it diced, on skewers. The Swiss have been known to make a kind of "dog jerky" by seasoning and drying unwanted pooches. The ancient Aztecs subsisted mainly on the meat of hairless dogs, which were fattened and consumed the way we eat beef today.

And speaking of beef—in most countries (including our own) nothing, from ear to hoof, goes uneaten. England is famous for its headcheese; that is, the meat of a cow's head, suspended in gelatin. Hungarians like to fry slices of calf's head in lard, and serve them with baked potatoes and tartar sauce. In Denmark, strips of beef tongue are combined with beets, apples, and hard-boiled eggs and served in a kind of Waldorf salad. Norwegians like to poach beef brains and the French like to cream them, while the Germans make a soup of diced brains called *hirnsuppe*. Stomach, lungs, cheeks, intestines, spleen, blood, and udders all are happily munched by adventuresome eaters around the world. When it comes to eating the unmentionable, however, the French take the *gâteau* (cake). They sometimes eat stuffed calves eyes.

Bon appetit!

Make-Your-Own Sundaes

You will need:

- A few quarts of assorted ice cream (Figure on one quart for every four people.)
- Chocolate syrup
- Butterscotch sauce
- Assorted chopped nuts
- Crushed pineapple
- Maraschino cherries
- Bananas, sliced
- Several cans of whipped cream
- Chocolate and rainbow sprinkles

Arrange sauces and garnishes around the tubs of ice cream. Provide ice cream scoops and dishes for the sundaes. And don't forget the napkins!

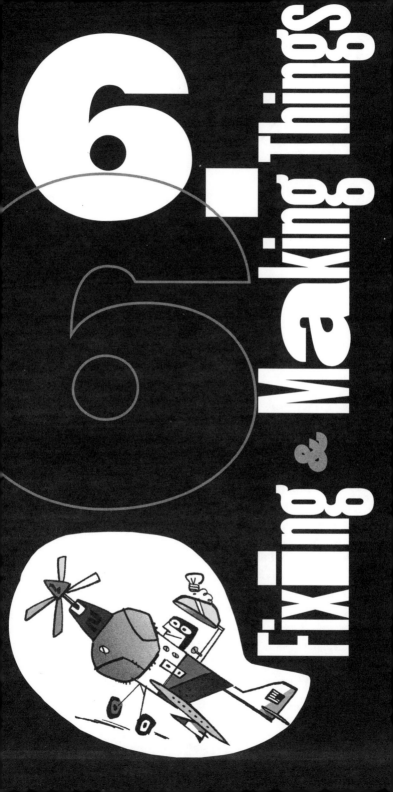

6. ■ Fixing & Making Things

Mr. Fixit!

A Basic Carpenter's Kit

A carpenter is never far from his tool kit. Here's what they carry (and you should, too).

■ **Box** or bag to keep tools in.

■ **Hammer** Like baseball bats and bowling balls, hammers come in different weights. Try a few out, and choose one that's not too heavy. A claw hammer (one with a two-pronged nail-removing "claw") is more practical than a ball-peen hammer (a rounded counter-weight on the other end of the business end).

■ **Nails** There are basically two basic kinds of nails—nails with flattened heads and nails without heads, or "finishing" nails. Nails are sold by length and weight and described in Old English penny weights—3d, 6d, 8d, and so on. The higher the number, the longer (and thicker) the nail will be. Always keep an assortment of nails in your kit.

■ **Phillips-Head Screwdriver** A screwdriver with a cross on the tip. Phillips-head screws are usually convex (curve out) rather than flat. This and the cross-shape make it easier for the screwdriver to grip the screw. Get a medium-size screwdriver with some screws to match.

■ **Slotted-Tip Screwdriver** This is a screwdriver that fits into the slots of flat-headed screws. Phillips-head screws are better for most jobs, but you'll need this, too. Get a medium-size screwdriver.

■ **Hacksaw** This is a good basic saw for most small carpentry jobs.

■ **Pliers** The most commonly used are slip-joint pliers. These pliers have square, toothed grippers and can be adjusted for wide or narrow jobs. Also, many come with wire-cutters attached.

■ **Clamp** The most useful kind of clamp is a C-clamp (so called because it's shaped like the letter). Clamps are mainly used for holding two pieces of wood together after gluing. A 3-inch, light-duty C-clamp should do it.

■ **Measuring Tape** Get a retractable, steel measuring tape rather than the folding wood kind. Ten feet is enough for most jobs. You'll be tempted, but try not to play with it too much—it can break.

■ **Combination Square** This handy tool has more than one use: it's good for measuring and marking lines as well as right angles. Also, it has a level—which comes in mighty handy when you're trying to decide where to hang that shelf.

■ **Sandpaper** Get a combination pack with coarse, medium, and fine.

If you're the kind of kid ...

who likes looking at beautiful tools, you should definitely send away for the Garret Wade catalogue. It's free. The address is: Garrett Wade, 161 Ave. of the Americas, New York, NY 10013.

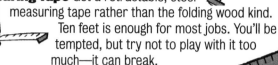

THE CARPENTER'S CREED

Measure twice, cut once. If you follow this simple creed you'll save yourself a lot of time—and wood.

Emergency Bike Repairs

Usually, your bike will break down when it's raining. It always seems to work out that way.

How to Change a Flat Tire on Your Bike

Two pieces of gear any regular bike rider should own:

- A patch kit, which costs $3 or less, and contains rubber cement, small pieces of sandpaper, and patches—usually 10 or so

- Tire levers, which are usually sold in groups of three, and also cost about $3 for a set.

Here's What to Do

- Move far off the road to repair the flat.
- Remove the tire from the bike.
- Make sure all the air is out of the tire.
- Locate the side of the tire that's opposite from the valve. That's where you'll be working.

- Putting your first tire lever on one side of the tire, pry gently. Be as careful as possible to avoid pinching the inner tube. Take the second tire lever and repeat the procedure about three inches away—on the same side of the tire. Keep repeating until one side of the tire is outside the rim.

- Pull the stem of the inner tube out of the rim. Remove the inner tube from the wheel. Leave the tire half on/off the rim.

- Very carefully run your finger along the inside of the tire to find and remove any sharp objects that might have caused the puncture.

Patching the Inner Tube

- Blow the inner tube back up. Listen carefully to hear air hissing out of the leak area. If you can't hear anything, dip the inflated inner tube into water, a section at a time, and look for air bubbles. That will be your leak area. Be sure to dry the inner tube thoroughly.

- Once you find the hole, use sandpaper to scrape all around the puncture area—clear about a one-inch radius.

- Apply rubber cement to the area. Let it dry for about a minute.

- Put the patch over the hole, making sure all sides of the patch are down smoothly. Press tightly against the patch area for a good minute.

- Wait another three minutes.
- Put enough air in the inner tube to make it firm—don't over-inflate.

Final Steps

- Stick the stem of the valve back into hole in the wheel rim.
- Put the tube back into the tire. Make sure tube isn't bunched up.
- Using the tire levers, tuck the tire back into the rim. Be extra careful not to pinch the inner tube.
- From a height of about two inches, bounce the tire all around to make sure it settles.
- Reattach tire.

Putting a Bicycle Chain Back On

There's no way to avoid getting your hands dirty with this job. If you have a ten-speed, put the chain on the smaller ring. If you don't have a ten-speed, lift up the back tire and move the pedals forward half a rotation to get them out of the way while you work. Replace the chain in this order:

- Thread the chain through the hub in the back.
- If you have one, thread the chain through the derailleur.
- Bring the chain to the top of the front pedal sprocket.
- Rotate the pedals slowly and the chain will fall into place on the sprockets.

Fixing a Leaky Faucet

Faucet Screw

Most faucet leaks are caused by bad washers. If you want to impress your dad, your mom, and yourself, fix it yourself! Let your parents know what you want to do, then:

- Turn off the water, either with the main valve or with the valve under the sink, so you won't get a gushing flood when you remove the faucet. This is a really important step. Don't skip it.

- Use a monkey wrench to unscrew the nut cap at the top of the faucet. Put a piece of cloth between the jaws of the wrench to keep from scratching the metal faucet.
- Pull or twist out the spindle.
- Loosen the screw that holds the old washer in place and remove the washer.
- Put in a new washer and replace the screw.
- Replace the spindle and tighten the cap of the faucet.
- After the faucet's tightened, turn the water on again at the valve.

Painting a Wall

The paint can will have directions—follow them! Some painting basics:

- Take off the old paint by scraping or with paint remover.
- Fill any cracks or holes with spackle. Spread it on with a spackle or putty knife. Let it dry completely. Sand the spackled part with fine sandpaper.
- Be careful not to overload your brush with too much paint each time you dip.
- Paint *with* the grain of the wood using straight, even strokes.
- Be sure the first coat is completely dry before you put on a second one.

Make a Twig Picture Frame

The size of the frame will depend on the size of the twigs you select. If you're making a square frame, all four twigs should be the same size. For a rectangular frame, you'll need two different-sized pairs of twigs.

- Put two same-sized twigs down and place the other two twigs across the first pair, making sure that the ends stick out to give it that Adirondack look.

- Apply a good, strong glue (Tacky Glue is great on wood) at the four spots where the twigs cross. Let the glue dry.

- Square lash the twigs together with cord or string, using a clove hitch to start and end each lashing. Use an everyday over-hand knot to finish.

- Glue a mounting board (which you can buy in any stationery, art supply, or five-and-dime store) or a sturdy piece of card-board (cut to the right size, of course!) on the back.

- Now glue a photo—or drawing—on the cardboard or mount-ing board and you've got a great gift or souvenir.

How to Tie a Clove Hitch

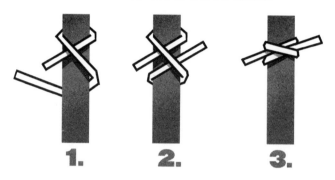

Make a Light Switch

Making your own light switch is a good way to learn how elec-tricity works. Here's what you need:

- A block of wood
- A 1-by-3-inch strip of copper*
- Hammer and several ¾-inch common (headed) nails*
- 3 feet of insulated lighting wire*
- A small light bulb in a porcelain socket*
- A six-volt lantern battery*
- A sharp knife or single-edged razorblade*

*You can buy all of these things in a real hardware store. A "housewares" store is not the same thing as a hardware store!

Here's What to Do

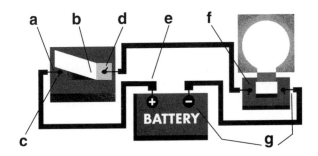

■ Cut the insulated wire into three equal pieces, each at least 12 inches long.

■ With your knife or razorblade, strip off about ½" of the insulation on the ends of each piece of wire.

■ Pound a nail part-way into the wooden block, near one end (a).

■ Nail the copper strip to the other end of the block, but don't pound it all the way in. The other end of the strip should be lying on top of the first nail. Bend the strip up, as shown (b).

■ Wrap the stripped end of wire number 1 around the first nail, then pound it down with hammer. This will secure the wire to the wooden block (c).

■ Wrap the end of wire number 2 to the second nail, then pound it securely in (d).

■ Attach the other end of wire number 1 to one of the battery's terminals (e).

■ Attach the other end of wire number 2 to one of the loosened screws in the light socket. Screw it down tightly (f).

■ Attach one end of wire number 3 to the second battery terminal, and the other end to the remaining light socket. Screw it down tightly (g).

■ Now you're ready to test out your light switch. Press down the bent copper switch until it touches the nail beneath it. When you do, the light should go on. If it doesn't, check to make sure that metal is touching metal at all of your terminals.

All of the light switches in your house work just like the one you've just made.

WOOD GLOSSARY

Lumberyard workers speak a kind of shorthand when describing cuts of wood. Here's a short glossary of common wood-words, so you won't feel stupid the next time you're at the lumberyard:

Clear Wood: A board without any knots or blemishes. Clear board is much more expensive than "common" board.

Solid Wood: Wood that isn't laminated (like plywood) or pressed (like masonite or press-board).

One-by-Four: Written as 1 x 4, this describes the thickness and width of a length of board. If you ask for a 6-foot 1 x 4, you'll get a board 6 feet long, 4 inches wide, and $^3/_4$-inch thick. The thickness of the board you get is always a little less than the measurement describing it. So, if you want a board that will be one inch thick, you ask for a five-quarter inch (written 5/4") board. What you'll get is a board that is one-and-one-sixteenth-inch thick. Don't ask why, that's just the way they do it.

Make a Cutting Board

You'll need:

■ A piece of solid hardwood, at least one inch thick. (Oak, poplar, or maple will do nicely.)

■ Coarse, medium, and fine sandpaper

■ Cooking oil and a rubbing cloth

Ask the lumberyard if they have some scrap wood you can use. If they won't give you any, ask them to cut off a one-foot piece from an untreated, $^5/_4$-inch board.

Once you have your board, it's just a matter of sanding and oiling it. Starting with the coarse sandpaper, rub off all of the board's surface irregularities. Next, use the medium and then the fine sandpaper. Your board should be very smooth on both sides, with no rough edges. (If you're using a tree round, though, leave the bark on.)

Pour some cooking oil on a rag and begin to work it into the wood. Remember, food is going on it, so don't use linseed oil or any chemically-treated oil on your cutting board. When the board is completely covered with the oil, let it sit for a few days; the wood will absorb even more. Wipe off any excess oil and voilà!, a cutting board.

A Multi-Purpose Plank

This looks easy, but you'll need to use all your carpentry skills to make it the right way.

A good, smooth plank can be used for all sorts of things: as a see-saw, a ladder, a slide, or a connecting bridge between two branches or buildings. Here's how to make your own plank, starting with a list of things you'll need:

■ A board of hardwood, like oak or maple. The board should be straight and free of any knots. Your plank needs to be at least 6 feet long and 9 inches wide, so ask for a length of clear (unknotted) 1 by 10. (You'll end up with a board 9¼" wide by ¾" thick. Remember, that's the way lumberyards do it.)

■ A wood rasp (a wood file)

■ A pack of assorted sandpaper

■ 3-foot piece of wood lattice, ¼" by 1" (You can buy this wood trim at a hardware store or lumber yard.)

■ A hacksaw

■ Phillips-head screw, at least 1¼" long

■ A Phillips-head screwdriver

■ Elmer's wood glue

■ Linseed oil and rags

The first thing to do is sand your plank. Using the wood rasp, file down all the sharp edges. Round the ends of the plank. Now, sand the entire plank—first with the coarse sandpaper, then with medium. Next, cut your lattice into four equal-sized strips. If your plank is 9 inches wide, make 4 seven-inch strips. (Leave one inch on either side of each strip). Sand the edges of each strip until smooth. Place your strips on the underside of the board, like this:

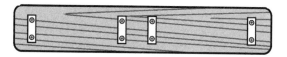

One strip should go near each end, and the two in the middle should have enough space for a fulcrum (the middle part of a seesaw) to fit between them. Glue the strips to the wood and let them dry. With a large nail, carefully make two pilot holes (starter holes so screws go in more easily) in each strip for the screws to go into. If you bang too hard with the hammer, the strips may crack, so go slowly! Screw in the screws.

Now it's time to "finish" the plank. Go over the whole plank with fine sandpaper, then put some linseed oil on a rag and work it into the wood to give it a super-smooth surface.

■ Make your plank a see-saw by placing it on a round log.

■ Hook one end onto a low wall or fence and use it as a slide.

■ Hook it between the branches of two trees, and make a bridge.

Tag-Sale Tinkering

f you like jigsaw puzzles, you'll love this. The idea is to take something apart, then figure out how to put it back together again. That's all, but it can be a lot.

Start with something easy, like an old ball-point pen. As you take it apart, lay it out piece by piece and (this is important!) draw or describe each component, noting down the order in which it was taken apart. When it has been completely disassembled, try to put it back together again. If your notes were good, you should be able to re-assemble it in the exact order that it came apart. Fixing the object isn't necessarily the idea here. (That comes later.) You just want to understand how the pieces go together.

Once you've mastered simple tinkering, you can go for bigger game. Wind-up clocks and watches, cameras and cassettes, telephones, fans, and bikes—any old thing that has removable parts. When working on electrical appliances, always unplug them first and never plug in a re-assembled electrical appliance without adult supervision. Note: don't tinker with anything that is still in use unless you're absolutely sure you can put it back together again. Of course, there are lots of things that can't be re-assembled again after they've been taken apart—anything with riveted or welded parts, for instance. But don't let that discourage you; you'll still learn a lot taking them apart.

Garage sales and thrift stores provide plenty of raw material for the serious tinkerer. Be on the lookout for devices that have simple, mechanical parts. Stay away from anything that is computerized, or has a circuit board. They can be taken apart, but you'll need a degree in engineering to put them together again.

It helps to see a picture of the item you're tinkering with. In your local library you'll find there are a number of books that have "exploded" line drawings of everyday household objects such as the pen shown below. Look under "science," or "household." You can also find visual dictionaries in the reference section of most libraries. Sometimes the manufacturers will send you this information for free.

THE TINKERER'S TOOL KIT

You'll find the following items indispensable:

■ A jeweler's set (This is a tiny screwdriver shaft with several equally tiny interchangeable heads. Available at most hardware stores.)

■ A flathead screwdriver

■ A Phillips-head screwdriver

■ Needle-nose pliers

■ An Allen-wrench set

■ A socket set

Around-the-House How-To's

A Basic Sewing Kit

It's a good idea, even for boys, to have a basic collection of things you can use to make sewing repairs.

Find a special box with a lid (a round metal tin, or deep cigar box, for instance) or buy a sewing box at a variety store. If you're making your own box, line it with felt. Here are some of the basic tools you'll need for your sewing kit:

- Fabric (not paper) scissors
- Spools of black and white thread, plus any other colors you may need
- A 60" plastic measuring tape
- An assortment pack of needles
- A needle threader (optional)
- A thimble or square of rawhide, for pushing needles through heavy material
- A box of straight pins

HOW TO THREAD A NEEDLE

Your thread should be about as long as your arm. If it's too long, it will tangle easily. Cut the thread on a slant (so it's less likely to ravel), then give the cut end a quick lick. Glide the slightly-damp thread through the eye of the needle. Make a small knot at the very end of the thread.

- A pin-cushion
- Assorted buttons

Tip: Always keep black and white threaded needles handy, for quick repair jobs.

HUCK AND SEWING

Even though he says his name is "Mary" and he's wearing a dress to disguise himself as a girl, Huck Finn is discovered to be a boy:

I had got so uneasy I couldn't set still. I had to do something with my hands; so I took up a needle off of the table and went to threading it. My hands shook, and I was making a bad job of it. When the woman stopped talking, I looked up, and she was looking at me pretty curious, and smiling a little. I put down the needle and thread . . .

Then she looked me straight in the face, but very pleasant, and says:

"Come, now—what's your real name?"

"Wh-what, mum?"

"What's your real name? Is it Bill, or Tom, or Bob?— or what is it?"

The woman explains how she saw through Huck's disguise:

"You do a girl tolerable poor, but you might fool men, maybe. Bless you, child, when you set out to thread a needle, don't hold the thread still and fetch the needle up to it; hold the needle still and poke the thread at it—that's the way a woman most always does; but a man always does 'tother way . . .

"Why, I spotted you for a boy when you was threading the needle."

How to Sew on a Button

1. Thread the needle and remember to knot the end of the thread.

2. Pierce the fabric from the underside and come up through one of the button's holes.

3. Go from that spot over the top of the button and come back down through any other hole; repeat until you've gone through each hole several times and the button seems securely fastened.

4. Finish up on the underside of the fabric by knotting and then snipping the ends of the thread.

Button

Needle

String

Fabric

Damage Control

Here's how to remove some of the worst kid-stains:

■ **Magic Marker out of upholstery:** Follow the directions on Capture spot remover or put some rubbing alcohol on a rag and blot the marks. Gently rub the area, until the color comes off on the rag. Keep moving to new sections of the rag, so you don't rub the color back into the fabric.

■ **Craft glue out of carpeting:** If the glue has completely hardened, you'll need to carefully cut it out with a small pair of scissors. If the glue is still soft, dampen a sponge and press it on the glue spot. Leave the sponge on the area for a while, then rub away the softened glue with a paper towel. Repeat until all the glue has been removed.

■ **Silly Putty out of upholstery:** With a knife, scrape off excess Silly Putty. Spray WD-40 on the area and let it sit for a few moments. Scrape again with the knife. Continue spraying and scraping, until the Silly Putty is gone.

■ **Grass:** Rubbing alcohol will take away the grass stain, but it may take away the color on the fabric, too. Test it first, on a hidden area of the material. After letting the alcohol soak in, flush it off with cold running water.

■ **Greasy stains (chocolate, pudding, gravy, etc.):** Lay the fabric—stain side down—on a folded paper towel and pour some cleaning solvent through the fabric, onto the towel. Change the towel often. Rub pre-soak stick on stained area and launder.

■ **Blood stains out of fabric:** Dissolve one teaspoon of white vinegar in two cups of warm water. Pour the solution on the stain, just before laundering. Rinse it in hot water, after a few moments. You can also try commercial pre-soak products, like Shout!.

■ **Pen marks out of fabric:** Different pen manufacturers use different inks, so you'll need to try a few different things here. First, run cold—then hot—tap water over the spot. If that doesn't work let the fabric dry, then try rubbing alcohol. Pour a small amount of alcohol on the mark and let it soak in. Rub the area with an old toothbrush. If that doesn't work, try acetone nail polish remover. (First, check to make sure the acetone doesn't affect the color of the fabric.) You can also try spraying some hairspray on the stain, if it's ball-point pen ink. Then rub it gently. Finally, there are several commercial spot removers on the market, like Energine, Capture, and Renuzit, to name a few. Good luck!

To receive a free stain removal booklet, call 1-800-Crayola or write:

> Consumer Services
> Binney & Smith Inc.
> P.O. Box 431
> Easton, PA 18044-0431

The U.S. Department of Agriculture publishes a free booklet titled "Removing Stains from Fabrics." Write to them at: U.S. Dept. of Agriculture, Washington, DC 20250.

How to Make a Bed

You'll need a fitted sheet, a flat sheet, and pillowcases.

■ Strip the bed and take off the old pillowcases. Put the old sheets in one of the pillowcases.

■ Put the pillows in fresh pillowcases.

■ Place the fitted sheet on the mattress.

■ Lay the flat sheet on top of the fitted sheet with its deep-hemmed end up and its "right" side facing down. The top of the sheet's hem should be level with the head of the bed.

■ Tuck the foot of the sheet under the mattress. (If using blankets, lay them on the top sheet, about a foot down from the head of the bed. Tuck in the foot of the blanket and sheet together, as described.)

■ Fold down the top of the sheet so the deep hem is now facing right-side up.

■ Tuck in sheet (together with blankets) on each side.

■ Place a comforter or bedspread over the sheets and arrange the pillows on top.

A MAKESHIFT FITTED SHEET

Place a flat sheet evenly on the mattress. Make a knot a few inches down from one corner and hook that corner over one corner of the mattress. Do the same with the other three corners.

How to Take a Good Picture

Whether you're using a disposable camera or a $10,000 Hasselblad, the same principles apply when it comes to picture-taking.

1. Have an interesting subject.

2. Make sure the subject is well-framed.

3. Have the right lighting.

Here are a few tips :

■ **A good picture tells a story.** It's one thing to take a picture of your friend's shoe. But if you get a picture of your friend's shoe right after he's stepped on a wad of chewing gum, your picture will be a lot more interesting. Even if it's a still life, try and have your picture convey more than one idea.

■ **Keep it simple.** Try not to have too much going on in your picture. If there are too many subjects doing too many things, there will be a "three-ring-circus" effect—the eye won't know where to go. Whatever your subject is—a person, a flower, a wad of gum—have a contrasting background. The background should either be lighter or darker than the subject. Your eye will naturally be drawn to a subject if it stands out against its background.

■ **Keep it natural.** A good picture doesn't look posed. When photographing people, give them something to do. If they're preoccupied, they won't look too self-conscious. Professional photographers always try to have some tricks up their sleeve when they go out on jobs.

■ **Don't center your subject.** Your picture will be more interesting if the subject is a little off-center. Also, try not to be on the same level as your subject, but shoot from a little above or below it. Angles and diagonal lines add excitement to a picture, so include them whenever you can.

■ **Get as close as you can to the action.** Your ability to get close to your subject depends on your camera's lens. Most automatic cameras don't feature close-up lenses, so experiment a little and discover just how close you can get without losing focus. When taking portraits, it's not necessary for the person's entire body to appear in the shot, but be careful to leave some space above the subject's head. If you don't, the picture will seem "crowded."

Avoid These Common Mistakes

■ **Tilted camera** In general, try to keep your camera at the same angle (not level) as your subject. Diagonal lines are dramatic, but a tilted horizon can make the viewer feel a bit queasy.

■ **Blurred image** This happens when the camera moves at the same instant the shutter opens. Unless you're taking pictures on the Tilt-a-Whirl, keep your camera steady.

■ **Bad lighting** Lighting is what separates the amateurs from the professional photographers. You don't need a lot of special equipment like they do, but you do need some basic lighting tips:

1. Don't shoot directly into the sun. If you do, too much light will hit the film, and your picture will be washed out.

2. Keep the sun out of your subject's eyes. When you're shooting people, the sun should either be to their left or their right. If it is directly behind you, your subject will be squinting. If it is directly behind them, you'll be squinting and your picture will be over-exposed.

3. Avoid the midday sun when shooting outside. When the sun is directly overhead, it casts deep shadows under the subject. This is especially important when you're taking pictures of people. Morning or afternoon light isn't as intense, and makes for a better picture. Bright, overcast days supply the best light for shooting outside.

4. When using an indoor flash, try to limit the number of objects in your shot. Concentrate on your main subject, and try to keep the background simple. When taking flash pictures of people (or animals) you can avoid the "red-eye" effect by directing your subjects' attention away from the camera.

Parts of a Camera

shutter button
view finder

film advance
flash bulb
focus ring
lens

How to Take Fingerprints

■ Use a stamp pad—black is the best color. If the pad's a little dried out, it will work better.

■ Make sure the fingers are clean and dry. Firmly roll the finger, from the tip to just below the first joint, back and forth over the pad, making sure the finger is well inked. Don't saturate the finger with ink; you want it to be covered thinly, but evenly.

■ Use the same rolling motion when you transfer the ink to the paper.

■ Even though no two people can have the same fingerprints, there are eight basic fingerprint patterns:

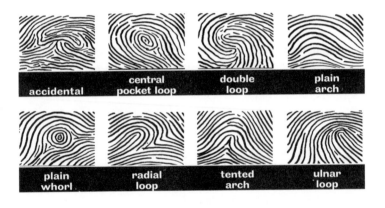

| accidental | central pocket loop | double loop | plain arch |
| plain whorl | radial loop | tented arch | ulnar loop |

PRINTS AS iD

In the 1800s a British scientist, Sir Francis Galton, concluded that fingerprints were means of positive identification. As a matter of fact, in parts of China and other Asian countries where many people didn't know how to write, single finger prints had long been used as identifying "signatures."

Another Englishman, Sir Edward Richard Henry, who was Inspector General of Police in Bengal, India, developed a way to classify fingerprints. Henry used a numerical formula to describe the different fingerprint patterns. In 1902 Scotland Yard adopted the Henry system and the United States followed in 1903.

If you want to make a file of different people's prints, just use a single finger—usually the right index (pointing) finger. Here's how you might set up a fingerprint file:

Right

PatternType
Name
Address

Index

PatternType
Name
Address

Fingers

Cool Things to Make

Make a Shrunken Head

Bring this out around Halloween-time.

- Get a large potato and core out two holes, for eyes. Put a marble in each hole.
- Cut two smaller holes, for nostrils.
- Gouge out a trough for the mouth and glue popcorn in it, for teeth.
- Cut two flaps of potato skin where the ears should be. Fold them forward (they'll shrivel nicely).
- Glue some unraveled black cord or corn silk on top of the head, for hair.
- Glue pieces of white or black thread on the nostrils and chin.
- Cut out a thin wedge from one cheek, then cross-hatch the gouge. This will shrink to make a nice scar.

Push the bottom of your shrunken head onto a sharpened stick or dowel. The longer it sits, the more it shrinks; the more it shrinks, the creepier it looks!

Here's Mr. Pumpkinhead

Sometimes you look at your friends and think you wish you had a really handsome companion, somebody who would make you look good by just hanging around with you. Here you are.

You'll need:

- A large pumpkin
- Two radishes
- A carrot
- An ear of regular or Indian corn
- Some parsley or corn silk
- A bell pepper sliced in half, lengthwise
- A carving knife

1. Cut out a disk around the stem of your pumpkin and remove it.

2. Reach in with your hand and take out all of the pumpkin's insides. (If you like them, save the seeds for roasting.)

3. Cut out two almond-shaped holes for eyes. Make them narrow enough for the radishes to fit inside.

4. Gouge out a small hole in each radish. (These will be pupils).

5. Wedge each radish into an eye-hole. Position the white "pupils" seem to be staring straight ahead.

6. Cut a round hole in the pumpkin for the nose. Push the fat end of your carrot into the hole.

7. Cut a trough for the pumpkin's mouth.

8. Cut off each tip of your corn cob and wedge the cob into the mouth hole. You'll probably have to adjust the size of your hole for the corn cob to fit into it.

9. Scoop out the seeds and membrane from the bell pepper halves. Place one of the pepper halves where the ear should go, with the cut half touching the pumpkin. With a felt pen, trace the shape of the pepper half. Cut out a trough for the pepper to fit into. Do the same on the other side.

A Sock Puppet

To make this easy puppet, you'll need:

- A grown-up's white athletic sock
- Felt, for eyes and hair
- Tacky glue
- Scissors
- A small paper plate
- Red construction paper

Here's what to do:

1. Cut an oval shape from the paper plate, as wide as your sock is. Fold in the middle.

2. Cut out a tongue shape from the construction paper.

3. Fold a 1" flap at the top of the "tongue" and glue it right under the fold of the plate.

4. Put the sock in your hand and form a "mouth" by putting your thumb at the heel and your other fingers in the toe.

5. Put glue on the back of the oval and glue it inside the mouth.

6. Cut out two round eyes from felt and glue them on.

7. Cut a long rectangle from the felt. Fringe both ends, leaving a "part" in the middle.

8. Glue the felt hair to the top of your puppet, at the part.

■ Make several puppets and put on a puppet show for your friends and family. Experiment with different color socks, eyes, and hair. Put on antlers, or a mustache. Make a frog or an alien. You'll have lots of fun thinking up ideas for sock puppets.

Scratch Building

Cannibalize your about-to-be-discarded old toys and put them together in new, interesting ways. Use whatever's at hand—old plastic dinosaurs, Hot Wheels, action figures, whatever!—and concoct a totally original creation. The only limit's your imagination. Remember what the evil kid did in "Toy Story?"

Scratch Model Making

The idea's the same as for the previous activity, "Scratch Building." Construct new aircraft using parts from different kits—just make sure everything's to the same scale. Use what you have at home or look for additional sets (and inspiration!) at tag sales.

Build Your Own Volcano

Make this outside!
You will need:

- Baking soda
- Vinegar
- Food coloring (red is best)
- Cup, spoon, pan

This really is an easy one.

1. Put the cup in the pan.

2. Pour ½ cup of vinegar into the cup. Add a few drops of food coloring.

3. Add 2 tablespoons of baking soda to the vinegar, and stir.

4. STAND BACK!

An Ear-Splitting Whistle

A really loud whistle is essential for calling friends, startling enemies, and flagging taxicabs—every boy should know how to make one. It's easiest to start with the four-finger method. Once you've gotten that down, you can switch to the single-hand whistle. If you get to be a real expert, you can whistle without using your fingers at all!

The Four-Finger Whistle

■ Take your two middle fingers and place them under your tongue. Curl the tongue into a U shape

■ Put your two "pointer" fingers next to your middle fingers, so the entire tongue is lifted and slightly curled toward the roof of your mouth.

■ Blow as hard as you can. You should hear a whistling sound coming from beneath the tongue (like the sound wind makes, rushing through a loose windowpane). If you do, that's the sound you're going for. If you don't hear it, try curling your tongue a little more, then a little less. If you still don't hear a whistling sound, reposition your fingers or lips slightly, until you do.

■ Practice. Practice. Practice. It may be days, or weeks, before you achieve an honest-to-goodness whistle. Just keep trying to make the whistling sound sharper and blow harder. Move your tongue a little. Move your fingers a little. Whenever you hear a "rushing" sound, go with it. At some point you'll surprise yourself with a really loud shriek. From then on, it will happen every time. It's a little like riding a bike: once you get it, you never forget it. When you've mastered the four-finger whistle, you can start to learn the two-finger whistle.

The Two-Finger Whistle

■ Put the thumb and middle fingers of your writing hand together.

■ Lift the tip of your tongue up. Blow—just as you did with the four-finger whistle. It'll be easier this time, but you'll still need to practice, practice, practice!

The Fingerless Whistle

This one is tricky (and a little hard to explain). Stretch your upper lip over your lower lip and blow down. Curl your tongue and move it around until you hear the whistling sound. (Note: some people can never whistle this way—it requires a very flexible tongue.)

Duck Call

This one's a cinch. All you need is a blade of grass and two thumbs. Almost any kind of grass will do, but you should choose a blade that's at least three inches long and a quarter-inch wide. Also, it should be sturdy and relatively flat.

■ Put your two thumbs together. There should be an almond-shaped space between the first and second joints.

- Now, take the blade of grass and trap it between the two lower joints of your thumb. Pull it up with your pointer fingers and hold it in place with the top joint.

- Put the grass up to your lips and blow.

To make a duck call, the blade needs to be a little slack when held between the two joints. The looser the blade is, the more slowly it will vibrate. The slower the vibration, the lower the sound. (If the blade of grass is stretched tight, it will make a high, shrieking sound.)

It may take some practice to get a good sound at first. If you're having trouble, try moving the position of the grass slightly, in relation to your lips. Also, play around with the tightness of the blade. (If it's too loose, it won't vibrate at all.) If you still can't get a sound, try another blade of grass.

How to Make a Willow Whistle

- Cut a piece of willow branch about the size of your middle finger, maybe just a little bit bigger.

- Make a little notch just like in the picture below.

- Cutting only the bark, not into the wood, make another cut all around the outside of the branch, about ¾" from the end.

- Now you want to loosen the bark and gently ease it off the branch—without breaking it. Here's what you do: Dip the wood in water and very, very gently tap on the bark with the shaft of your pocket knife. Repeat the dipping and tapping until the bark is soft enough to slip off the branch without breaking. Put the bark aside, but don't let it break!

- Make another cut in the wood as in the picture below.

- Gently slip the bark back on again and blow.

Making a Quill Pen from a Feather

The only tool you'll need is a penknife, or an X-Acto-type knife.

■ **Make sure your feather** is big enough. In the old days, goose and turkey feathers were most commonly used.

■ **Clean the feather.** If you've found a fresh feather, scald the tip in boiling water for a couple of minutes. You want to make sure the end is clean so the ink will flow freely. The Dutch used to put feather tips in hot sand (140 degrees in the oven) for a few minutes.

■ **Let the feather dry** overnight before you cut it.

■ **You have to clean off the cuticle** at the end of the shaft. The cuticle is the clear, smooth, hard and shiny part. Use your thumbnail or a dull kitchen knife to peel away the cuticle.

■ **On the backside** of the feather you'll see a long dent. Using your thumbnail or a dull blade, scrape the *pith* (soft, squishy stuff) off the dent.

■ **Cut the tapered tip** of the quill off. Scrape out any pith you find inside the quill.

■ **Using your X-Acto** or penknife, cut a scooped-out area on end of the quill. It should be about one-half inch from the tip.

■ **Now, cut a slit down the middle** of the feather tip. Make the cut as straight as you can.

■ **Very gradually shave** or cut the quill tip on each side until it forms a V at the center slit.

■ **Use an emery board** to smooth any rough spots.

■ **Soak your pen in water** for about 15 minutes before you use it—every time. This will keep the nib (or tip) flexible and less likely to break. Dip your pen into the ink and write or paint away!

DID YOU KNOW . . .

American colonists made a red ink from the strained juice of boiled cranberries.

Beanbags

Here are two instant beanbags you can make on the spot.

■ **Ziplok Beanbag** Fill a small Ziplok bag with dried beans. Seal it, then put that bag into another Ziplok bag, upside down. Seal, and cover the seal with masking tape.

■ **Sock Beanbag** Put a handful of beans into the toe of a sock. Twist the sock and turn it inside-out. Twist the sock again and turn it inside-out. Keep turning the sock, until you run out of sock.

Homemade Punching Bag

Before you even get started with this, you'll have to get permission from your parents to screw a good strong hook into the top door frame (called the overhead lintel) of your room—or whichever room you plan to use. If they say no, then ask if you can hang the bag from a garage rafter or something.

Next, you'll need an old cushion from a couch or a chair and about six feet of strong cord or rope. Tie the rope very tightly around the cushion about a third of the way down, which will divide the cushion into two parts.

With the other end of the rope make a non-sliding loop, and stick the loop over the hook. Make sure the cushion is hanging at the right height for easy punching.

PRIZE FIGHTING RULES

If you decide to take your pillow-punching skills to the ring, you should know what's against the rules. Here's what *not* to do:

1. Hit an opponent below the belt.
2. Hit an opponent when he is down; hit him when he is getting up after he has been down.
3. Hold an opponent or purposely maintain a clinch.
4. Hit with the inside or butt of the hand, wrist, or elbow.
5. Hold with one hand and hit with the other.
6. "Flick" or "slap" with an open glove.
7. Wrestle or rough on the ropes.
8. Fall down without being hit (take a "flop").
9. Use the kidney punch (purposely punch at the part of the body over the kidneys).
10. Use the pivot blow or the rabbit punch.
11. Butt with the head or shoulders or give the "knee."
12. Use abusive or profane language (if the referee hears it).
13. Disobey the referee after having been warned.

Fly a Kite

Kites are more fun to fly if they're kites you've made yourself. Follow the pictured instructions: You should always fly a kite in an open area, away from power lines and antennas.

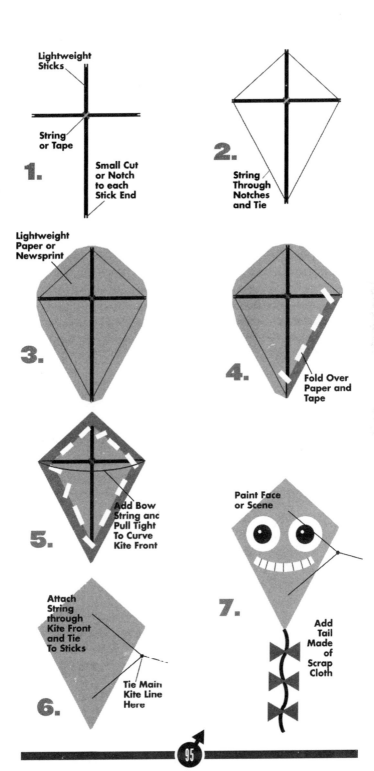

1. Lightweight Sticks
String or Tape
Small Cut or Notch to each Stick End

2. String Through Notches and Tie

3. Lightweight Paper or Newsprint

4. Fold Over Paper and Tape

5. Add Bow String and Pull Tight To Curve Kite Front

6. Attach String through Kite Front and Tie To Sticks
Tie Main Kite Line Here

7. Paint Face or Scene
Add Tail Made of Scrap Cloth

FOUR WORLD WAR TWO FIGHTER PLANES

British Spitfire

German Messerschmitt BF 109

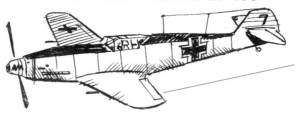

American P-51 Mustang

Japanese Zero

BALLOON MESSAGES

Send up a balloon with the following message attached to it (glued on to the balloon, or tied on to a string).

If you find this balloon, please send a postcard with your location and the date found to:
(Your name and address).

Send up a bunch of balloons and see how many responses you get, and how far the balloons go.

Make a Parachute

■ Cut a square of plastic.

■ Cut two pieces of string, each one-and-one-half to two times longer than the diagonal of the plastic.

■ Cut each piece of string in half, to make four lengths of string. Tie, tape, or glue a piece of string to the first corner, as shown. In the same way, put a piece of string on each remaining corner.

■ Tie the bottoms of the strings together and attach a metal nut to them (as in the picture below).

■ Fold up the parachute so that it's as small as possible and release it from a ladder—or something even higher, like an airplane!

Paper Cutting

Here are five trillion things to do with folded paper and scissors.

How to Make Your Own Paper Cup

Use paper that is glossy on one or both sides—like wrapping paper or a magazine cover. Make sure the paper can be sharply creased.

■ Start with a square piece of paper. To make a square from a rectangular piece of paper, fold the right-hand corner of the paper over until it lines up with the left side, forming a triangle. Cut or tear off the extra paper (a).

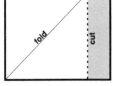
a.

■ Make your square into a triangle by bringing two corners together (b). Make sure they line up exactly. Crease.

■ With the base (long side) of the triangle down, bring the left corner to a point in the middle of the right side (c). Crease. Now do the same thing with the right side (d).

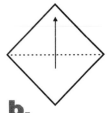
b.

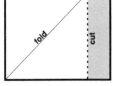
c. **d.**

■ Fold the front flap forward (e). Turn cup over and fold the other flap down (f).

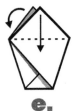
e.

f.

Make a Pyramid

These make great ornaments. It's also a fun way to kill some time if you finish your test before everyone else. You'll need paper, scissors, and glue.

Making a triangle: Start with a rectangular piece of paper.

1. Fold paper in half, lengthwise (a).

2. Open the paper and fold the lower right-hand corner up to a point in the middle of the paper (b).

3. Bring the right-hand corner down, until it's even with the diagonal bottom line (c).

4. Unfold the paper and cut on the folded lines (d). This is the shape you'll need to make your pyramid.

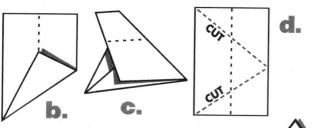

b. c. d.

CUT
CUT

Making the pyramid: At this point, it's useful to label the corners of your triangle (e).

5. Fold X to the middle of the opposite side (f). Unfold.

6. Fold Y to the middle of the opposite side. Unfold.

7. Fold Z to the middle of the opposite side. Unfold. Now you should have the fold lines of a smaller triangle inside your large triangle (g).

8. With X pointed up, fold the bottom of the triangle so that it looks like illustration h.

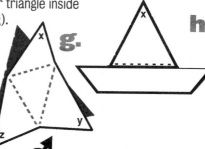

e. f. g. h.

9. Unfold, and do the same with the other two sides of your triangle (i).

10. Now unfold the paper so it looks like figure j.

i.

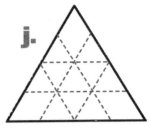

j.

11. Number the different triangles and make dark lines, as shown in figure k. Cut on the dark lines.

12. Fold triangle 1 over triangle 5 and glue (l).

13. Fold 2, 6, and 7 to make the base of your pyramid and glue them down.

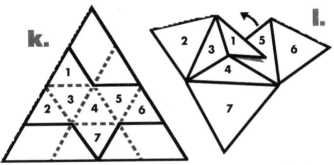

k.

l.

Now that you know how, try to make another one, this time without numbering the small triangles.

Make a Cube

As one kid says, "You do a lot of folding, but it's pretty easy."

1. Start with a rectangular piece of paper and make it into a square

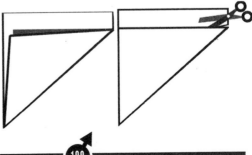

2. Fold another triangle (a, b).

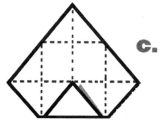

a.

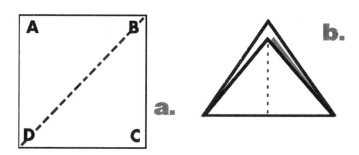

b.

3. Fold one corner to the center fold line, then unfold. Repeat with the other 3 sides (c).

4. Fold one corner to crease line A, then unfold. Repeat with the other three sides (d).

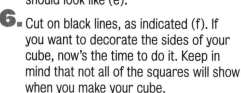

c.

d.

5. Fold each of the corners to the crease closest to it, then unfold. When you're finished, your paper should look like (e).

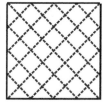

e.

6. Cut on black lines, as indicated (f). If you want to decorate the sides of your cube, now's the time to do it. Keep in mind that not all of the squares will show when you make your cube.

7. Fold into a cube. (There's no special way to fold your cube; any way you fold it, you'll get a cube!)

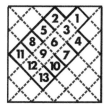

f.

Now that you've got a cube, here are a few things you can do with it:

Make a 6-Sided Picture Puzzle Make four cubes. Cut six different square pictures into quarters and paste one quarter of each picture on a facet of each cube. Do each block of four at a time, then mix them up and try to put them back together again.

Make a 4-Color Cube Puzzle This was a favorite game of colonial American children. Make four cubes. Color each facet of your cube according to the diagrams. The colors are red, white, blue, and yellow. (The box on the far right side of each diagram indicates the bottom of each cube.) The object of the puzzle is to line up all four cubes so that *each one* of the colors is on all four sides in each row. (The end colors count.) It can be done, but it's hard! If you want to know the solution, go to the library and check out *Colonial American Crafts: The School* by Judith Hoffman Corwin.

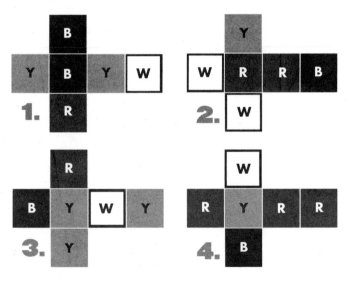

A Two-Color Lantern

Make a bunch of these out of brightly colored paper, and string them along a path to your house.

You'll need two different colored sheets of construction paper, scissors, and tape.

1. Take one sheet of paper and roll it, widthwise, into a tube. Tape shut at top and bottom.

2. Fold the other piece in half, lengthwise (a).

3. Make a series of slashes at the foldline, leaving borders at each end (b).

a.

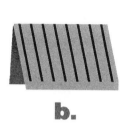

b.

c.

4. Open paper and wrap it around the other tube. Press it so the vents stick out (c).

5. Tape the ends of the lantern together.

6. Tape to the inner tube. Decorate the borders.

7. Glue some yarn to the top, to hang your lantern.

Make a Paper Box

Use origami paper, or a piece of wrapping paper, cut into a square.

1. Fold paper in half, then fold in half again. Unfold.

2. Fold all four corners to the middle (a).

3. Fold two sides of the square to the middle, making a rectangle. Unfold (b).

a.

b.

4. Turn, and fold the other two sides to the middle (c).

5. Unfold (d).

6. Now, open two corners (e).

7. Fold to the middle on the creased line (f).

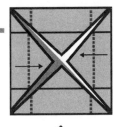

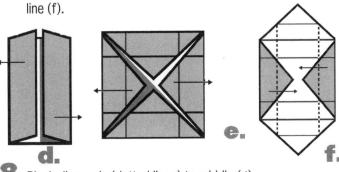

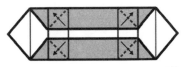

8. Pinch diagonals (dotted lines) to middle (g).

9. Fold flap down (h).

10. Repeat on other side (i).

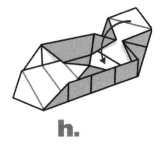

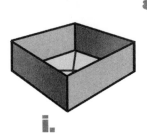

Nested Boxes

The perfect way to give a small, valuable gift to someone very special.

■ You'll need a pack of origami paper, a pencil, ruler and scissors. If you can get a pack of different-sized paper, great. Otherwise, get a pack of the largest (8") size. Take the top sheet and put it aside. This will be the lid of your largest box. Take the next two sheets and with a ruler, measure ½ inch from the edge on all four sides. Trim off sides. Take the next two sheets of paper and measure 1 inch from the edges. Trim. Continue cutting off the edges, ½" more each time, until you've reached a 5" square. (You only need to make one of these.)

■ Make a box, as directed previously, with the largest paper. This will be the lid for your nest.

■ Repeat all the box-making steps with all your paper.

■ Now it's time to nest your boxes. Starting with the largest box, put all your boxes one inside the other. Put your present in the smallest box, then put the next-smallest box on top of it, for a lid. Continue to put bigger lids on each box until you run out of lids. Turn your nest-of-boxes over. Decorate the top box.

More Paper Fun

The Expanding Paper Tell your friends that your body can pass through a single sheet of paper. If they challenge you to prove it, do this:

1. Take a sheet of paper and fold it in half, lengthwise.

2. Cut along the horizontal lines, as shown in the right-hand picture. Cut *through* the fold for the lines that meet it. Cut from the outer edge *toward* the fold for the lines that meet the edge, but don't cut all the way across into the fold!

3. Open your paper up and lay it flat.

4. Cut on the fold-line *inside* the paper, leaving about an inch on each end (as shown below—cut only on the middle black dotted line). Do not cut the the gray fold-lines on either end!

5. Open the paper up and step through it.

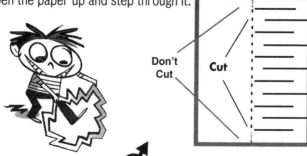

Shrinking Paper A perfect way to send a secret message.

1. Take a piece of paper and write your secret message on it.

2. Fold paper in half, lengthwise (a).

3. Fold in half again (b).

4. Take one corner of your folded strip and fold it to the edge, making a triangle (c).

5. Continue folding into triangles (d) until you get to the last triangle before the top.

6. Tuck top flap into the pocket of the triangle below it (e).

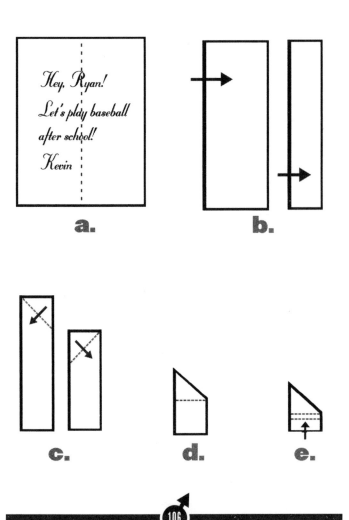

Hey, Ryan!
Let's play baseball
after school!
Kevin

a.

b.

c.

d.

e.

Printmaking and Painting

You can use everyday materials to make stamps for printing.

Cookie-Cutter Potato Stamps

Here's a variation on the old potato print. You'll need some cookie cutters with small designs: hearts, stars, and animal shapes work well. Take a large potato and cut it in half. Blot the potato juice with a paper towel.

Press the cookie cutter into the potato, to a depth of about one-half inch. With a small, sharp knife, cut away the background from your design. Remove the cookie cutter. Pour a small amount of poster paint into a mini tray*. Put the roller into the tray and roll it back and forth until the paint is evenly distributed on the roller. Roll the paint onto the potato and stamp it on a piece of scrap paper. Adjust the thickness of your paint, if necessary. Now, stamp your design on stationery or craft paper.

*Most paint and hardware stores sell "mini-tray-and-roller" sets. They cost less than $3.00 and are definitely worth buying if you plan to do much printing. If you don't have one of these, just paint with a brush, directly onto your stamp.

Glue Stamps

Draw a design by gently squeezing white glue onto a piece of corrugated cardboard. The small squeeze-bottles work best. Let your design dry overnight. Put some poster paint in a mini tray, spread it out and apply the roller to the raised glue design. Place some paper on the stamp and gently smooth it with your hand. Remove the paper and let dry.

Styrofoam Stamps

Take a good-sized piece of Styrofoam (not the small chips used in packing) and with a serrated knife, cut several blocks from it. With a ballpoint pen or nail, scratch a design onto one face of the block. If you're writing, be sure to do it backwards—you can double-check your writing by holding your stamp up to a mirror. Spread the paint evenly with a roller and make your prints.

Rubberband Monogram

Collect some wide (⅛") rubberbands. Cut them into strips and arrange them so they spell out your initials. When you're satisfied with the way your monogram looks, take a block of wood and lightly paint it with rubber cement. Make a border around the edges of the block, then place your monogram inside the border. Be sure to place your initials on the block backwards, from right to left! Roll paint onto your stamp and use it to ID books and other paper possessions.

Splatter Painting

You can make interesting prints with a wooden frame, some screen-door wire, a toothbrush, and paint or ink.

■ Pick up an orange crate* from a supermarket, and take the bottom slats off. Staple or nail a piece of screen wire to the top of the crate.

■ Place a leaf or some other familiar-looking object on a piece of white paper. Set this paper on newsprint, then put the frame over it.

■ Dip the toothbrush in paint or ink and rub it back and forth over the screen wire. The paint will splatter on the uncovered part of the paper. Remove the leaf from the paper and you'll end up with a reverse-stencil print.

*or make a simple wooden frame by nailing four 2' x 4's together.

Egg Coloring

Here are two different ways to color hard-boiled eggs. Remember, if you're dyeing an egg more than one color, always go from a lighter color to a darker one.

Coloring with Crayon The hard-boiled egg should still be slightly warm. Using only one color, draw a design with a crayon on the egg. Take a tissue and rub off any extra wax. Put on a second color. Rub off. Continue with your design, putting on one color at a time. It's easy to make a rainbow using crayons. Put a stripe of yellow in the middle and layer stripes of green, blue, and violet going in one direction; orange, red, and purple in the other.

Dyeing Eggs with Natural Colors Use saffron or turmeric for yellow, beet juice for pink, red cabbage for violet, and boiled onion skins for golden brown.

EGG-TALK

Put the word "egg" in front of every vowel in a word.

"Degg-ooh yegg-ooh wegg-ant tegg-ooh gegg-o tegg-ooh thegg-a megg-all?"

"Negg-o. Legg-ets gegg-o tegg-ooh megg-eye hegg-ous egg-instegg-ed"

Translation: "Do you want to go to the mall?" "No. Let's go to my house, instead."

Patent Your Invention

If you think you've invented something totally unique, you may want to look into patenting it. When you patent something, you're registering it with the United States Patent Office—for a fee. This protects you from having your idea stolen. Once it's patented, you can sell your invention outright to a manufacturer or work out a royalty agreement.

The first thing you have to find out is whether your invention is unique. Either you can hire someone (a patent attorney) to find out for you or you can do it yourself. Many large cities have patent libraries, where a record is kept of all past and pending (not-yet approved) patents. Patents are filed by category.

Once you're pretty sure your idea is unique, the next step is filing a patent application. There's a fee for filing an application, and no guarantee your application will be accepted. Still, if your invention is really terrific, it's worth it.

In addition to the fee, you'll need:

■ A document that describes your invention and explains how it is both unique and useful.

■ A technical drawing, which shows how it works.

■ A notarized statement that you're the one and only inventor of your idea.

PATENT INFO

To find out about requirements and fees for patenting your invention, write:

> Superintendent of Documents
> U.S. Government Printing Office
> Washington, DC 20402

Ask for their guide, "Patents and Inventions: An Information Aid for Inventors."

7.

Things TO DO INdoors

Sometimes, a rainy day can be a great gift—a chance to catch up on a favorite book or build a favorite model. But there are other days when a day indoors can just be . . . BORING!

Games for Groups

Beanarino

A good one when you're stuck indoors.

■ Get three different-sized containers (for example, a cup, a cereal bowl, and a larger shallow bowl) and make a nest of the dishes.

■ Put the dish nest on the table, about four feet from the edge. Grab a handful of dried beans.

■ The object is to toss the beans into the bowls. If the bean lands in the biggest bowl, that's worth one point. If the bean lands in the middle-sized bowl, it counts for two points. And if the bean lands in the smallest bowl, it's worth three points.

■ Each game is ten innings long, and each player tosses five beans in each inning. The beans are thrown from behind the table (four feet away), one at a time, into the target. A player is allowed to lean over the table as much as he wants to, as long as he doesn't touch the table.

■ After each player throws his five beans, add up his score, write it down, and take the beans out of the dishes. Beans count only where they finally land. The player who scores the most points wins.

DOIK!

IQ

This is that little game—sometimes called "Hi-Q"—they sometimes put on tables in coffee shops. You can make your own.

Making the Board You'll need a block of Sculpy, Fimo or any air-drying clay and a box of toothpicks. Roll the clay into a 4" square. It should be at least ½" thick. Put a sheet of tracing paper over the pattern, right, and trace the dots onto the paper.

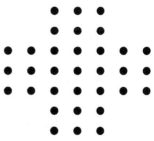

Put the tracing paper over the clay. With a toothpick, poke a hole through each dot into the clay. Bake or air-dry it until it's hard.

Setting Up the Game Cut the toothpicks down to peg size and put a peg into every hole but the middle one. The object of the game is to "jump" your pegs, one at a time, until only one peg is left on the board. You can jump horizontally or vertically, but not diagonally.

Your first move will be over a peg and into the hole. Take the peg you've just jumped and put it aside. Now two holes are available and you have a choice of several possible moves. Continue jumping until you can't make any more moves. If more than one peg is left on the board, you lose. If only one peg is left on the board, you won.

Heads, Bodies, and Tails

■ Each player will need a pen and a piece of paper. Have each boy fold his paper into three sections.

■ Draw a head on the top third of the paper. It can be human or animal or anything you want—as long as it's a head. Draw a neck, making sure it extends into the second section.

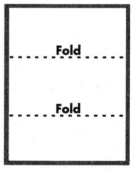

■ Fold your paper so that just the second section is visible and pass the paper to the person on your right. (The person on the left will pass his paper to you.)

■ In the second section, draw a body and arms—if your creature has them. Make the waistline extend into the third section. Fold the paper again—this time so that only the third section is visible—and pass it to the right.

■ Now it's time to draw the third section. The "tail" could belong to a fish or a reptile or a mammal or a Martian! When you've finished the drawing, fold your paper closed and pass it one last time. Everyone will get a laugh when they open up their composite drawings.

Charades

This is another game, like hopscotch, that many people play without actually knowing the official rules. Here they are:

You need at least six players for charades as well as scraps of paper, pencils and a watch.

Divide the group into two teams. (If there's an extra boy, he can be the group leader and timer.) Give each boy a scrap of paper. Each player writes a familiar word or phrase. Almost anything goes. For example, you could write down a movie, a TV show, a book title, a song, the name of a popular band, or an advertising slogan. Since the object is to stump the other team, every player tries to make his word or phrase as difficult as possible.

The papers from each team are collected and put in separate piles or bowls. A player from Team 1 is given a paper prepared by someone from Team 2. The first player must silently act out the word or words on his paper. His teammates try to guess what he's "saying." He is given four minutes. If his teammates correctly guess the message he's acting out, that team gets five points. If the time runs out, they get no points.

Whether or not the first team scores, the play now goes to the second team. A player from Team 2 is given one of the papers prepared by Team 1 and four minutes to act out the word or phrase. The teams take turns acting and guessing. Each boy gets a turn to pantomime a message for his teammates to guess. After all of the papers have been acted out, the team with the most points wins.

■ Before the game starts, the whole group needs to decide on gestures to represent the category each message falls in (a book, movie, song, etc.) They should also make up different gestures to signify "word," "group of words," and "syllable."

■ If you have a long word that's hard to act out, try breaking it down into syllables. For instance, "uncomfortable" could be broken down as "un" (the first syllable of onion), "come," "fort," and "table."

Camouflage

Here's a fun indoor game for a group.

To set this game up, gather together about twenty small household items. Some possibilities might be a penny, a nail, a button, a sticker, a safety pin, a crayon, a walnut, a toothbrush, etc. When selecting your items, try and pick out things that will fade into the background of the room where they'll be hidden. (Try to pick out some things that are the same color as your sofa or rug, for instance.) Make a list of the items, and draw a blank line next to each item. Each player will need his own copy of the list. Now, go around the room and "hide" your items in plain sight. For instance, you might put a black button on top of a black book or place your walnut in the dirt of a potted plant.

Now you're ready to play. Assemble the group and hand each boy a checklist. The players must find each of the listed objects. Tell them the items are not hidden, but they are camouflaged. When a player spots an item, he should check it off the list and write where it is hidden in the blank space, but *no player may move an object or in any way give away its hiding place*. The first person to check off all the items gets a special prize, but the hunt continues until everyone is finished. It's not a bad idea to give everyone some sort of reward when he finishes. (If some kids are really having trouble, one of the finishers can help by telling them if they are "hot" or "cold.")

Murder!

This is a game to be played in the dark of night.

Each player draws a piece of paper from a paper bag. After looking at his paper, each person crumples it up and tosses it back in the paper bag. Most of the papers are blank. But one paper has "Murderer" written on it and one other says, "Detective."

The Detective leaves the room and the lights are turned out. Make sure the room is very dark. The rest of the players move around in the middle of the room until the Murderer puts his hands on somebody's throat. That person screams and drops to the floor.

Turn the lights on and call in the Detective. The Detective asks questions, which everyone has to answer honestly— everyone but the Murderer, that is, who's allowed to lie.

By asking clever questions, the Detective tries to figure out who the Murderer is.

Put Him in Jail

It's like Hangman, except instead of hanging him, you put him behind bars.

One person's the guesser and the other person's the jailer. The jailer thinks of a word, say, "PEOPLE." The jailer makes six dashes on the sheet of paper; one dash for each letter of the word he's thinking of, like this:

— — — — — —

Next, the jailer draws the jail cell:
Now it's time for the guesser to begin guessing. If the guesser guesses the letter E the jailer fills in all the Es.

   E — — — — E

But if the guesser guesses R, or some other letter not in the word, the jailer starts to put the guesser in jail. With the first wrong guess, the jailer draws the guesser's head near the top of the cell. With the second wrong guess, the body; third wrong guess, a leg; with the fourth, the other leg; fifth, one arm; sixth, the other arm.

After seven wrong guesses, the jailer locks the guesser in jail, by drawing bars across the guesser. The jailer then picks another word and the game starts all over again. But if the guesser guesses the word in time, he becomes the jailer.

Snake

You'll need a large, open room with an uncarpeted floor for this game. (A gym is perfect.)

With chalk, draw a large circle on the floor. One person is the snake. The others are its prey. Everyone stays inside the circle; if you go outside the circle, you die. The snake lies on the floor, with his arms stretched in front of him, his hands clasped together. He propels himself by wiggling forward on his belly or thrashing from side to side. The snake tries to catch prey by tagging it with his hands. If he tags someone, that person becomes a snake, too. Eventually, there are as many snakes as there are prey.

BiG SNAKE

This game is played the same way, only when someone is tagged, he joins the snake by holding him by his ankles. The two-man snake needs to work together to catch prey. If a third person is tagged, he becomes a new snake. A fourth joins the third, and so on. You can play two-man, three-man, or four-man snake.

Off! On!

This is one of the easiest games to set up, but it's not so easy to play. You'll need a rug (or a piece of material) and a lot of kids.

Put the rug in the middle of the room. Pick someone to be the caller. When the caller yells "Off!" everyone has to jump *on* the rug. When the caller yells "On!" everyone jumps *off*. Anyone caught *off* the rug at the command of "off" is out; anyone caught *on* the rug at the command of "on" is out. The last kid left, wins. That's it.

The caller tries to trick people. For instance, he may call a long string of "ons," then suddenly throw in an "off." Also, the caller speeds up and slows down his commands. This game can go on for a long time.

Marbles

■ **Ringer:** With chalk, make a large circle on asphalt. Make two crossing lines, dividing the circle into quarters.

■ **To decide which player goes first,** have each kid shoot a marble towards the center. The player who gets closest to the center cross, goes first. The next closest goes second, and so on.

■ **Next, each player places his marbles,** in an L shape, on the outside of each of the four quarters. If there are only two players, place your marbles across from each other in two of the quarters. Each player should have an equal number of marbles to start with.

■ **The first shooter aims his boulder** from any spot on the edge of the ring. Any marble that he knocks out of the circle belongs to him. He keeps shooting until he fails to knock a marble out. Now, it's the second shooter's turn. He also keeps shooting, until he misses. The game continues in this way, until all the marbles have been knocked out of the ring. The player with the most marbles at the end wins.

MARBLE GOLF

This game needs to be played on tightly-packed dirt. With a stick, draw a large circle on the ground. In the very center, dig a hole (If you want, you can put a small cup in the hole.) Scatter the marbles evenly, inside the circle. Each player takes turns trying to knock marbles into the cup. When a marble is knocked in, the player gets to keep it. The first player keeps shooting, until he misses; then, it's the next player's turn. The game continues until all the marbles have been knocked into the hole.

CRACKED MARBLES

Here's a fun thing to do around the campfire or at a cookout. You'll need some marbles, a cup of cold water, and an old wooden spoon. Heat a marble in the coals of a dying fire. When the marble is somewhere between very warm and hot, scoop it up with the spoon and drop it in the cup of water. The marble will crackle inside but stay intact. If your marble is too hot, though, it will crack into pieces. You'll probably need to experiment with a few marbles, until you get it right.

Broom Hockey

Simple—brooms for hockey sticks, boxes or laundry baskets as goals, and a Nerf, or other lightweight ball, for a puck—but better clear this with a parent first.

Formula One Dice Race

David Weir, a former Formula One race car driver, adapted this game from the "after-supper-races" which were once a shipboard activity for Atlantic steamship crossings. He likes to play this game with his son, Gregory.

You'll need:

- A pair of dice (or one die, for a shorter track)
- An oval track, made with dominoes or cards laid end-to-end.
- Matchbox racing cars (one for each player)

1. Mark one card (or domino) "Start" and the one behind it "Finish."

2. Have every player choose a car.

3. Driver 1 rolls the dice, then moves his car one card (or domino) according to the number rolled. (For instance, if he rolls a seven, he moves his car to the seventh card in the track.)

4. The other players do the same, in turn. You can have a one-, two-, or three-circuit race, depending on how long you want to play the game. The first car to reach the "Finish" card wins.

Thumb Wrestling

Object: To pin you opponent's thumb before he pins yours.

The Rules: Hook the fingers of your right hand with your opponent's fingers, keeping the thumbs straight up in the "ready position" until someone shouts, "Go!" You have to keep your fingers hooked, no matter what. It's a pin if you hold your opponent's thumb down for a count of three.

Chestnut Fights

Find a good-looking horse chestnut—hard, not too big, or too small—and drill or pound (with a nail and hammer) a hole through the center. Run a shoestring through the hole and tie a knot at the bottom. Your fighting chestnut is now ready.

The Fight: It's your chestnut against your friend's chestnut. One of you holds the top of his shoestring so that the chestnut dangles down. The other person wraps his shoestring around his index finger, leaving enough room (a couple of inches of shoestring) for momentum to build when he wields his fighter chestnut. He supports his chestnut with his outstretched thumb, then flicks/smashes it against the dangling chestnut.

■ The flicking/smashing maneuver takes a lot of work to perfect—it has to be done quickly and like you mean it. The person doing the smashing keeps going until he misses.

■ Once that happens, switch places. After a while, one of the chestnuts will start to crack (Careful! It can be the hitter as well as the hittee.) The game ends when one of the chestnuts is killed—smashed off its string.

A truly great chestnut survives five such fights, and then may be retired.

A Pointer: Various methods have been tried to harden chestnuts and increase their durability. In some places shellac has been outlawed. If you do try to harden your fighting chestnut, be careful not to leave it too brittle.

Acting Up

It's fun to put on plays for friends and family. Try making a play out of one of the stories or books you already know or love.

Peter Pan, by Sir James M. Barrie, makes a great play. You, of course, are Peter Pan or Captain Hook. If you have younger brothers or sisters, they can play the other kids.

Start with chapter three, where Peter comes into the children's bedroom, to find his lost shadow. Peter's shadow can be a piece of black chiffon tied to fishing line. (Have someone make it fly around the room by pulling on the line from offstage.) Tinker Bell can be the light of a flashlight shining on the wall. If you have some tinkly chimes, play them whenever Tinker Bell speaks.

Other suggestions: *Robin Hood Stories, King Arthur Tales,* fairy tales, or musicals like the *Wizard of Oz.* It's fun to act out the Greek myths, too.

Make an Orchestra

You don't need to spend big bucks to make music; all you need are a few household props, and your imagination. Here are some ideas to get you started:

Water Chimes: Gather as many tall drinking glasses as you can. Ideally, they should be identical. Line the glasses up next to each other, but they shouldn't be touching. Get a set of measuring cups and fill a pitcher with water. Pour ¼ cup of water into the first glass. Pour ½ cup of water into the second, ¾ cup into the third, and one cup of water into the fourth glass. Continue filling the glasses, ¼ cup more each time, until you run out of glasses—or room for water. Strike the glasses lightly with a metal spoon. Each one will chime a different sound. If you have a piano, try to determine the notes your glasses are chiming. (You may add or take away water from a glass, to get a higher or lower sound.)

A Tom-Tom: To get the proper sound, you'll need a square of rubber inner tubing. You can buy an inner tube new, but it's expensive; see if an automotive shop will give you an old one. With a can opener, remove the bottom from a large coffee can. Drape a square of inner tubing over the top of your drum. Wrap a length of bendable wire around the inner tubing and twist it until the rubber is held in place. Pull the inner tube taut on all sides and keep twisting the wire, until your drumhead is tight and smooth.

Drumstick: Use a 12" dowel, ½" in diameter. With a wood rasp, taper the tip, then sand it smooth.

A Wok Cymbal: Pick up a used wok at a thrift store (there's always at least one). Hold it by a shoelace strung through its handle and hit it with a large metal spoon. You'll get a nice, loud, crashing sound.

Spoons: To play the spoons you have to be sitting. Hold two identical spoons in one hand, back to back. Slip your index finger between the spoons. Tap the spoons against your knee, then against the open palm of your other hand. The spoons will rattle and clatter as they dance between your knee and your palm.

Sandpaper Blocks: Tear a sheet of fine sandpaper in half and wrap each piece around a wooden building block. Glue or tack the sandpaper in place. Rub the two blocks together for a scritchy-scratchy sound.

A Comb Kazoo: Fold a strip of waxed paper around the teeth of a standard hair comb. Put your lips lightly on the paper and hum. You'll hear a buzzing sound. Make a kazoo section for your orchestra.

A Wine Bottle Tuba: Tuck in your lower lip and blow down through the neck of an empty wine bottle. You'll get a deep sound, like a foghorn. Experiment with different tones by putting water in the wine bottle. Have two tubas in your orchestra and "tune" one to C and the other to G for an oom-pah-pah sound.

A Garden-Hose Trumpet: Cut a length from an old garden hose and, pressing your lips together, blow into it. You'll get a trumpet-y *blaaat* sound. If you move the hose back and forth while blowing, you'll sound like a stampeding elephant!

A Shoebox Banjo: Cut a hole into the lid of a sturdy shoebox. Tape the lid down and stretch four rubberbands around the length of the box. Experiment with different rubber band thicknesses. See if you can "tune" your rubberbands to G, C, E, and A. Pluck the strings of your banjo over the hole.

CHARLIE'S HOMEMADE JUG BAND

Your band can have drums, a banjo, and some sort of horn.

Drum: You can use pots and pans, and pot lids for cymbals. Plastic buckets make a good sound, too. Wooden spoons make good drumsticks, or you can cut down wooden dowels to the right size. A hat box is great for a bass drum, if you can find one.

Banjo: Take a shallow basin (preferably metal), attach a thin wooden board for a neck. Then take string or wire and pull it really taut. Connect it to the bottom of the basin and top of the wooden board.

Bass: Just make the banjo on a larger scale and you'll have a bass. You can also make a washtub bass by attaching a string—heavy-duty fishing line works pretty well, and so does light wire—to the top of a broom handle. Attach the other end to the bottom of a washtub. Place the washtub face-down on the floor. Put the bottom of the broom handle on one edge of the tub bottom and pull it so the string's tight. Pluck the string. It'll make a different note depending on how tightly you pull the string.

Horn: A kazoo with a paper funnel at the end works well as a trumpet. A paper-covered comb makes a good sound, too.

A Tin-Can Telephone

Take two tin cans and poke a hole in the bottom of each one with a nail. Stick a long piece of string or heavy-weight, monofilament fishing line through the hole in each can and tie a button on the end to keep it from being pulled through the hole. Stretch the "wire" between the cans as tightly as possible. One talks while the other listens!

Making Semaphore Flags

As long ago as the 1500s, naval vessels communicated with each other using a code based on signal flags, called semaphore. Here's how to make your own semaphore flags.

For one set of flags:
You'll need two sticks, each about 2' long, two big pieces of heavy white paper, red paint or markers, and thumb tacks.

An official semaphore flag is 18" square. Measure and cut the paper into two 18" squares.

Divide the square in half diagonally by drawing a line from the upper right hand corner to the lower left hand corner.

Using your marker or paint, color the upper triangle red.

Attach the flags securely to the sticks with thumbtacks, about six tacks per stick. Make two sets of flags so you and a friend can signal to each other.

Semaphore Code

Note that A is also the number 1, B is 2, and so on, through J, which equals 0. If you want the other person to know you're sending a number, take the "numeral" position before transmitting the number.

There are also special positions for "error," "attention," "answering," and "end of word."

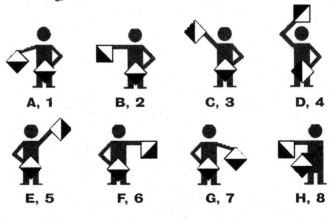

| A, 1 | B, 2 | C, 3 | D, 4 |
| E, 5 | F, 6 | G, 7 | H, 8 |

I, 9 J, 0 K, 7 L, 8

M N O P

Q R S T

U V W X

Y Z Numeral

Attention End of Word Error Answer

It's in the Cards

Hearts

Up to seven people can play this game.

The object is to get rid of all the hearts you're holding in your hand, and to keep from getting new ones. In the end, the player with the least number of hearts wins. If, however, a player has managed to pick up *all* the hearts, he wins the game. (This is called "shooting the moon.")

The cards are dealt evenly to all of the players. If there are any leftover cards, they are placed face down in the middle of the table. The player to the left of the dealer leads by putting down a card. The players to his left must then put down a card of the same suit. The player who puts down the highest card of that suit must take all of the cards—which is called "a trick." (He must also take the leftover cards, if there are any.) If a player has no cards of the leading suit, he may then put down any card he likes. This is the time to get rid of any hearts or high cards, because a trick may only go to the highest card in the leading suit. The boy who gets the trick leads again. The game continues in this way until all the cards have been played.

What Beats What in Poker?

Poker: a great way to double your allowance, if you can get your dad into a game. Here's the list, from the best poker hand down to the lowliest. For example, a straight flush beats four of a kind, and four of a kind beats a full house, and so on.

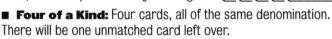

■ **Straight Flush:** Five cards in numerical order and all of the same suit. If you have an ace, king, queen, jack, and 10 of the same suit, that's called a royal flush, the best poker hand you can get.

■ **Four of a Kind:** Four cards, all of the same denomination. There will be one unmatched card left over.

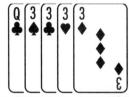

■ Full House: Three cards of one denomination, and two cards of another denomination.

■ Flush: Five cards all of the same suit (for example, all diamonds, all spades, all hearts, or all clubs). The cards don't have to be in sequence, or order.

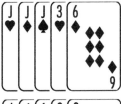

■ Straight: Five cards in sequence, but not all of the same suit.

■ Three of a Kind: Three cards all of the same denomination, and two unmatched cards.

■ Two Pair: Two cards of one denomination, two cards of another denomination, and one unmatched card.

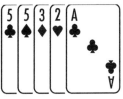

■ One Pair: Two cards of the same denomination, and three unmatched cards. A higher pair always beats a lower pair.

■ High Card: Five unmatched cards. If no one has any of the above, whoever has the highest card (Starting, from the top, with A K Q J, 10 9, etc.) wins.

WHY ARE ACES AND EIGHTS CALLED THE "DEAD MAN'S HAND"?

Because that's the hand that Wild Bill Hickok was holding when he was shot in the back!

A Card Game You Can Make

The name of the game is "Authors." Count out 52 cards from a package of 3"x5" index cards. Divide your "deck" into thirteen sets of four cards. Think of thirteen authors you've heard of, and some books that he or she has written. (You can also use playwrights, poets, or movie directors.)

Take the first card from the first set and write the name of an author in large letters near the top of the card. Above the author's name, write the title of one of his books. Under his name, write the names of three other books he has written. Above the author's name on the *second* card in the set, write one of the three other books he has written. Under his name, write the names of the other three. Repeat with the third and fourth cards in the set, putting the name of a different book at the top of each card. Prepare each of the remaining twelve sets in this way, using a different author for each set of four.

After you've made all 52 cards, shuffle them and divide them up between three to six players.

The object of the game is to collect as many sets as you can. When it's a player's turn, he might ask one of the other players, "Do you have *Billy Budd* by Herman Melville?" If that player is holding the card, he must give it to the asker. If he gets the card he asks for, the first player takes another turn. If he's holding three other Herman Melvilles, he puts all four cards down on the table, saying "I have a book." If a player *doesn't* get the card he asks for, it's the next player's turn.

Index Card Gymnastics

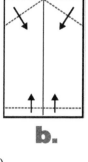

- Take a 3" x 5" index card and fold it in half, lengthwise.
- Unfold, and fold two corners to the middle (a).
- Fold up the bottom, as pictured (b).
- Fold both sides to the middle (c).
- Fold the top over, at dotted line (d).
- Turn the card over and fold the bottom up (e).
- Press down at the x and the card will do a somersault! (f)

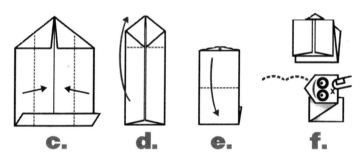

Two Good Card Tricks

Trick One

You'll need a table and a tablecloth.

- Display four overlapping aces on the table. After your audience takes a look, whisk the cards together and stick them in the middle of the deck.

- Ask someone in the audience to shuffle the cards. Show the audience you don't have any cards in your hands or up your sleeve. After the cards have been well shuffled, ask the shuffler to put the deck on the table.

- Invite the audience to come and hunt for the aces. They'll only find three—the ace of diamonds won't be in the deck. Pick up the deck and whack it on the table, saying, "I knocked the ace through the table!"

- Lift up the tablecloth and show everyone the missing ace.

Here's How You Do It:

The trick is that the audience never really saw four aces on the table—the ace of diamonds was hidden all along. The cards you showed at the beginning were three aces and the nine of diamonds.

Arrange the cards so that an ace is on each side of the nine, and the audience can see just the central diamond, as shown.

Make sure the audience doesn't look too closely at the cards when you're beginning the trick. And as soon as you can, push the cards together and put them in the deck.

Trick Two

■ Hold up four spread out kings. Push the kings together and put them on top of the deck of cards, which you should be holding in your other hand. Lift the top king off the pile, show it to your audience and say, "I'm putting the first king on the bottom of the deck." Then do so. Without showing the next card take it off the pile and announce, "The next king goes in the middle of the deck." Put it in the center and do the same thing with the following card, but make it very obvious that the third card is not close to the card you have just placed in the middle of the deck.

■ Take the fourth card, show it to the audience, and say, "I'm keeping this last king on top of the pile." Cut the cards and put them on the table. Ask someone from the audience to cut the cards again.

■ Now say something like, "You've seen me put kings in different parts of the deck. The deck has been cut twice—once by someone from the audience. Now I'm going to bring the kings together." Hit the cards with your fist, and ask someone from the audience to look through the deck: all the kings will be together.

Here's How You Do It:

Take the four kings and two jacks out of the deck. Put the two jacks behind one of the kings. Make sure the jacks are absolutely hidden behind the king—keep the edges flush.

When you fan the four kings at the beginning of the trick, make sure the king with the hidden jacks is the second card from the right as you spread the cards. Be careful not to show the jacks! When you turn the cards over and bring them together, this will be the order of the cards: king, jack, jack, king, king, king.

Put these cards on top of the deck. Pick up the first card—a king—and show it to everyone in the audience before you put it on the bottom. Since the next two cards are jacks, make sure you don't show them as you stick them in the middle of the deck. Even if the audience gets a glimpse of the cards, they'll assume they're kings, since jacks are picture cards, too.

After the jacks are safely buried in the deck, show the audience the next king, but tell them it's the last king. With the first cut of the deck, the king that's on the bottom of the deck will be brought on top with the other three kings, putting all the kings together. The next cut (from the audience) should put the kings somewhere in the middle of the deck. **Good luck!**

Pitching Cards

Two people, a deck of cards, and a hat—that's all you need for this one!

Divide a deck of cards into red (hearts and diamonds) and black (clubs and spades) suits. One player uses red cards, the other black cards.

Put the hat upside down on the floor. Pick and mark a place about five feet away from the hat. Each player takes turns pitching cards. Three cards are pitched on each turn. On the last pitch, only two cards are pitched.

When no more cards are left, count the number of cards that made it into the hat and you'll have a winner.

Rainy-Day Fun

Cookin' Up Fun

Here are the recipes. Now it's up to you.

Snowp: Mix equal parts Ivory Snowflakes and water. Beat with an egg-beater until stiff. *Warning*: snowp looks and spreads just like cake frosting.

Bubbles: Mix together 2 cups of clear liquid dishwashing detergent, ¾ cup of Karo syrup, 6 cups of water, and (if you have it) a few drops of glycerin. Mix well, and use it just like the stuff you buy in the tiny bottles with the little wands.

Silly Putty: Fill a plastic food container one fourth of the way up with white (Elmer's–type) glue. Add a few drops of food coloring, and stir. Add some liquid laundry starch until the container is half full. Stir again. (The mixture will begin to solidify and cling to the spoon.) Add more starch, until the container is almost full. Take the putty out and knead it with your hands until it is soft and rubbery. Drain off any extra liquid. To keep it pliable, store the Silly Putty in a Ziplok bag.

Gloop: In a plastic food container, combine 1 cup of white glue with ¾ cup of hot water. Set aside. In another bowl, combine one tablespoon of Borax with ½ cup of hot water. (Borax can be found along with laundry powder in most supermarkets.) Add half the Borax solution to the glue container and knead for a few minutes. Add the other half and continue kneading, until the mixture solidifies. Drain off any extra liquid. When it is not in use, store the gloop in a Ziplok bag.

Permanent sculpting sand: Measure 4 cups of sand, 2 cups of cornstarch, and 2½ cups of water into an old pot and heat on a low setting until the mixture becomes thick. Sculpt, and let your creation air-dry. Extra sand may be stored in a Ziplok bag.

Stained glass: Measure ¼ cup of hot water into a cup. Add several drops of food coloring, and stir. Gradually, add 2 packages of plain gelatin to the water, stirring as you do. When all the gelatin has dissolved, pour the mixture into two plastic food container lids. Allow it to dry overnight. The "stained glass" can be cut into different shapes with scissors. *Hint:* After a few hours of drying, shapes can also be cut out with cookie cutters.

Scented stained glass: Follow directions as above, but use flavored and colored Jell-o instead of gelatin.

Growing a Crystal Garden

You will need:
- Charcoal briquettes
- Salt
- Bluing (sold in laundry-detergent section of store)

- Ammonia
- Food coloring
- Small glass jar, cup, spoon, measuring spoons

Put a couple of charcoal briquettes in a small glass jar. In a cup, mix together 1 tablespoon salt, 1 tablespoon water, 1 tablespoon bluing, and 1 teaspoon of ammonia.

Pour the mixture over the charcoal briquettes. Sprinkle a few drops of food coloring on top.

Put the crystal garden in a safe place and watch it grow.

Two Yo-Yo Tricks

Sleeper: This is the trick where the yo-yo stays in one place, or "sleeps," while it's spinning.

Hold the yo-yo in your hand, palm up. Now bring your arm up to your shoulder, just like you're making a muscle.

Snap your hand downward, while at the same time relaxing your hand so the yo-yo will land gently. What you're trying to do is reduce the friction between the axle of the yo-yo and the string. If there's too much friction, the axle will grab at the string and start its return spin back into your hand.

If you're able to reduce the friction, your yo-yo will sleep. The next thing you'll have to figure out is how long to let the yo-yo sleep before you make it come back to your hand. That's something you'll learn with lots of practice.

WHO INVENTED THE YO-YO, ANYHOW?

The yo-yo comes from the Philippines, where it started out as a weapon. Early Philippine jungle inhabitants tied vines or animal sinews (tendons or muscles) around grooved rocks, and used these to knock animals—or human enemies—on the head. If they missed with the first throw, they could yank the rock back with the vine or sinew, and try again.

"Yo-yo" comes from a Philippine word meaning "to return."

Walking the Dog: To walk the dog, first you have to be able to throw a fast sleeper. The faster your sleeper, the longer you can walk your dog.

After throwing a fast sleeper, very carefully swing the yo-yo out, making sure it lands gently. The force of the spin will make the yo-yo walk along the floor or ground, with you trailing behind it.

As with the sleeper, you have to make sure to tug the yo-yo back into your hand before it stops spinning.

Internet Surfing

If you get your parents' permission, you can explore the Internet for games, pictures, sounds, movies, and freeware. Use a search engine such as WebCrawler or Magellan, for example, and put in the keyword for a subject you are interested in.

Pictures: Say you want to get the logos for college sports teams. Type the keyword "sports," the name of the college you're interested in, and/or the college's nickname (Example: "Wolverines"). This should get you mighty close to the logo.

Sounds: Type in the subject you like and the word "sound" and/or "audio." One fun thing to look for is downloads from your favorite cartoons and movies.

Movies: When looking for movie clips, your best bet is to type in the subject you like and the word "QuickTime." QuickTime is the most common way movies are stored on the Internet. You can also try "mpeg."

Freeware: Freeware is software available on the Internet and, believe it or not, it's free. You'll find games, programs for doing art and movies and for creating animation, among many other things. When you're searching, put in the word "freeware." This word should give you a list of sites that offer free programs.

Before you download anything, make sure you have an anti-virus program! You can download a free one called SAM DISINFECTANT.

On-line Lingo & Faces
Once you get on the Internet you're sure to see some of these abbreviations:

IMHO: in my humble opinion

LOL: laughing out loud

ROTFLOL: rolling on the floor laughing out loud

BTW: by the way

B4N: bye for now

FWIW: for what it's worth

<g> grin: This lets the person you're "talking" to know you're kidding about something.

You're also likely see some of these faces (turn your head sideways), made with keys on the keyboard.

:-)   :-D

;-)   :—(

These are called "emoticons," a word made from two other words—"emotion" (because the little faces show how you're feeling) and "icon" (because icons are small symbols used in place of words).

If you need help with your homework and you're on America OnLine, type in the keyword "homework." Teachers are standing by to help. You can also find homework help on the Internet by typing "homework" into a search engine.

Tracking the Weather

Make a calendar for the current month, giving each date box plenty of room. If you have an extra calendar with big date spaces, that's fine, too. Draw a line through each date square, dividing it in half.

Either read the newspaper prediction for the next day's weather or watch the same meteorologist every night on TV. In the top half of the date's space, fill in the next day's prediction. You can draw a picture (sun, cloud, rain), write the word, or simply list the predicted high and low temperatures. Use the bottom half of each date to draw or write in what actually happened, weather-wise, each day.

At the end of the month, tally up the number of times your prediction source was wrong. You can write a letter to the person to share your results if you want to.

RAIN GAUGE

The official rainfall is determined by the amount of rain that falls in one cubic inch of space.

You can make your own accurate rain gauge. You'll need a 12" beaker—available at a hobby shop or chemistry supply store. If your beaker isn't marked, get nail polish and label it yourself. Measure it out in ¼" segments.

Next, wire the beaker to a small board. Make sure the wire isn't too tight—you have to be able to get the beaker in and out when you empty it.

Now attach the board (nail or wire it) to a pole or fence post that's totally exposed to the sky on all sides. After each rainfall, check (and empty) the beaker-gauge.

For a free science catalog that sells beakers and lots of other science supplies, contact:

Edmond Scientific Company
Science Division
101 East Gloucester Pike
Barrington, NJ 08007-1380
Phone: 1-800-728-6999
M.–F. 8 AM–8 PM, Sat. 9AM–4PM
Fax: 609-547-3292
E-mail: scientifics@edsci.com

Get the Lay of the Land

Make a map of your neighborhood, using the private names you've given various locations. (For example, if you call the house two blocks over the "mean German shepherd's house," that's the name you'll put on your map.) If you make a map of the route you take to school, put in the shortcuts and show which neighbors' yards are best avoided.

Commonly Used Map Symbols

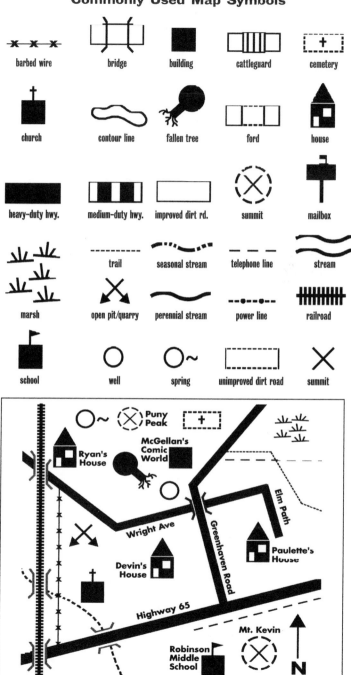

barbed wire	bridge	building	cattleguard	cemetery
church	contour line	fallen tree	ford	house
heavy-duty hwy.	medium-duty hwy.	improved dirt rd.	summit	mailbox
marsh	trail / open pit/quarry	seasonal stream / perennial stream	telephone line / power line	stream / railroad
school	well	spring	unimproved dirt road	summit

Sample Map

Puny Peak

Ryan's House

McGellan's Comic World

Wright Ave

Devin's House

Greenhaven Road

Elm Path

Paulette's House

Highway 65

Mt. Kevin

Robinson Middle School

N

Design Your Own Sports Teams and Leagues

Create a football, hockey, baseball, or basketball league. Look at a map and pick cities within your state, the country, or even the world—it's your choice. Give the team an appropriate name, say, "Topeka Tornadoes," and go to work!

Here's what you might need for each sport:

Football: Helmet and team colors

Hockey: Jersey and logo

Baseball: Cap and logo

Basketball: Logo, jersey, and shorts.

You can do this on a computer if you have an art program. Copy the cap or helmet, for example, and then paste it each time you want to create a new team.

Be an Armchair Traveler

You can get great books, pamphlets, brochures, and maps from foreign countries by just asking for them! Here's the way to get the mail rolling in:

First, find some travel magazines. Check the periodical (newspapers and magazines) section of your library. Since periodicals often can't be checked out, bring a pen and a notebook with you. In the back of each travel magazine, you'll find a section that offers free brochures from travel agencies, suggesting exotic places to visit.

Write down their addresses (or 800 numbers, if they have them) and ask for whatever they're willing to send you. In addition to travel agencies, you can also get information from local and foreign governments. Each state in the U.S. has a department of travel and tourism, and most countries do, too. Ask the librarian to show you how to find addresses for these. Also, ask for the out-of-town phone books—every city and town has a Chamber of Commerce, and you can write them and ask for promotional materials. Travel agencies and bureaucrats are eager to tempt you with pictures, maps, bumper-stickers, decals or postcards—all for the asking, and a stamp.

Collect cities, states' and countries. Trade with your friends. See how many different islands you can get, or how many countries in each continent. So, sit back and wait for the mail to come rolling in. Your friends will be surprised when they see the kind of mail you're getting—and they'll be impressed with your stamp collection, too!

Get a FREE beginners stamp collection packet from:

Junior Philatelists of America
P.O. Box 850
Boalsburg, PA 16827

Connect the Dots

Here's a fun strategy game:

You and your opponent both share the "board." Take a piece of paper and draw 16 dots, arranged like this:

```
•   •   •   •

•   •   •   •

•   •   •   •

•   •   •   •
```

In this game you take turns drawing a connecting line between any two dots. In turn you may connect *only* two dots. You can put your line anywhere; it can be horizontal (straight across) or vertical (up and down), but not diagonal (slanted).

The object of the game is to make as many small squares as you can, within the large square. If you connect the fourth line to make a square, you "capture" a box. Then you get to put your initials in the box, and take another turn. The winner is the boy who has claimed the most boxes at the end of the game. This game is a little like chess, because you need to think a few moves ahead to win. Try not to be the one to put the third line on a box; you'll be setting up your opponent to score.

If you want to play longer, make a square with 36 dots—six rows of six dots.

DUNGEON

First, you need to find a "dungeon." It should be the scariest place in the playground. Also, it should be near (but not touching) a fence.

The game is basically tag. One player (the Black Knight) tries to tag other players (white knights). The Black Knight can tag you anywhere on the playground except the fences and safety surfaces (black rubber mats under swings and slides, for example). If the Black Knight tags you, you have to go to the dungeon. White knights can free fellow knights by climbing along the fence to the dungeon. The Black Knight tries to keep people from getting on the fence and tries to catch them between the fence and dungeon. If you get dungeoned three times, you're *It*.

Hide and ...

"My dad works at a store that sells sports equipment and clothes. Sometimes I have to wait there a long time for him to finish with customers. To keep from getting bored, I pretend that I'm an escaped prisoner and the customers are guards (or Nazis). I like to hide very quietly in the racks of clothes, so they won't see me."

Wordplay

Use these expressions to impress your teachers and friends:

1. You're pressing upon my neural transmitters in a deleterious manner. (Translation: You're getting on my nerves.)

2. I beg to differ. On the contrary . . .
   (Translation: You're wrong! It's like this . . .)

3. Please forgive my oblivescence.
   (Translation: Sorry. I forgot.)

4. I am currently experiencing a eudaemonistic state.
   (Translation: I'm so happy!)

5. Would you please reiterate that statement? I was experiencing omphalokepsis.
(Translation: What'd you say? I wasn't listening.)

6. Although I covet his leiotrichous condition, I would readily eschew his lentiginous epidermis.
(Translation: I wish my hair were straight like his, but I'm glad I don't have his freckles.)

7. I fear that you have been less than forthright and obfuscated veracity.
(Translation: You lie!)

FYi

- If a word ends in "mania" it means *madness*.
- If a word starts with "philo" or ends in "phile" it means *love of* or *a lover of*.
- If a word ends in "ocracy" it means *a government of*.
- If a word ends in "ology" it means *the study of*.
- If a word ends in "mancy" it means *a way of predicting the future*.

Tongue Twisters

Everyone knows how hard it is to say "toy boat" ten times in a row real quickly, right? Once you've mastered that, try these:

- A cup of coffee in a copper coffeepot
- Six gray geese in a green field grazing
- Six slick slim saplings
- Six thick thistle sticks

Three Good Codes

Monk's Code

This is good, safe code, and it takes a little effort—but it's worth it. The Monk's Code was invented about 500 years ago by a German monk. You will need two code books—one for yourself and one for your code partner. A notebook is fine, but try to get one small enough to slip into your pocket, so it can be hidden easily.

Here's how it works: Each letter of the alphabet has its own page in the code book. There will be a list of words and simple phrases under every letter. For example:

A	B	C	D
near the	over	yesterday	the cat
underneath	I am	pretty old	goes to
3:30	under it	now	school
he said	let's go	woods	Why not?
once before	tonight		

Now, suppose you want to spell out the word "bad." Pick a word or phrase from the B page, then one from the A page, and finally one from the D page. Here are a couple of ways the word "bad" could be written out, using this code.

 *I am near the school.*

 *"Let's go," he said. Why not?*

Both code books will have twenty six lists like these, one for each letter of the alphabet. Try to pick words that go together, so the message written out in code makes some sort of sense. The longer your lists for each letter, the better your code will be. But, unfortunately, a good list for each letter also means it will take you a while to decode messages.

Only people who have code books will be able to understand the message, making the Monk's Code one of the safest there is.

HiDiNG A CODE BOOK

The best hiding place is an unexpected one. Tape your code book to the bottom of your waste basket, then put crumpled paper over the code book. A small code book can be hidden in the pocket of a jacket or coat that's hanging in your closet. Cut a square hole in the middle of an old book to make a secret hiding area for your code book.

And if your enemies are closing in and you need a foolproof hiding place, you can always send your code book to yourself in the mail. That will give you a couple of days breathing room to find a new, secure hiding spot.

First-Word Code

Suppose you want to send the message, "Let's play baseball after school," but you don't want that message falling into the wrong hands. Just write what looks like an ordinary note—but pick the first word of each line very, very carefully.

For example:

> Charlie,
> Let's study together later, okay? No time to
> play today, since I want to do well on the quiz.
> Baseball will have to wait, I guess, until
> after I've learned all the spelling words.
> School comes first!
> Reuvy

Pretty crafty!

Morse Code

People don't send message by telegraph anymore, which is what Morse Code was invented to do, but there are lots of other uses for this code. A message can be tapped out on a wall, beaten on a drum, whistled out, blinked out at night with a flashlight, or flashed with a mirror in daytime, using the sun.

Here's how Morse Code works: Each letter of the alphabet has a signal made of dots and/or dashes. Dots are short, and dashes are three times longer than dots. No matter how you send your message, by flashlight or by tapping, this will always be true.

Just count to 1 for a dot and to 3 for a dash.

Morse Code

A • —	J • — — —	S •••	1 • — — — —
B — •••	K — • —	T —	2 •• — — —
C — • — •	L • — ••	U •• —	3 ••• — —
D — ••	M — —	V ••• —	4 •••• —
E •	N — •	W • — —	5 •••••
F •• — •	O — — —	X — •• —	6 — ••••
G — — •	P • — — •	Y — • — —	7 — — •••
H ••••	Q — — • —	Z — — ••	8 — — — ••
I ••	R • — •		9 — — — — •
			0 — — — — —

Samuel Morse, the inventor of Morse Code, also came up with a way to memorize the code:

A Ag-ainst	• —	J Ju-ris-dic-tion	• — — —	S Se-ver-al	•••
B Bar-ba-ri-an	— •••	K Kan-ga-roo	— • —	T Tea	—
C Cont-in-ent-al	— • — •	L Le-gis-la-tor	• — ••	U Un-i-form	•• —
D Dah-li-a	— ••	M Moun-tain	— —	V Ve-ry va-ried	••• —
E (short)	•	N Nob-le	— •	W Wa-ter-loo	• — —
F Fu-ri-ous-ly	•• — •	O Off-ens-ive	— — —	X Ex-hi-bi-tion	— •• —
G Gal-lant-ly	— — •	P Pho-tog-raph-er	• — — •	Y Youth-ful and fair	— • — —
H Hu-mi-li-ty	••••	Q Queen Kath-a-rine	— — • —	Z (two long, two short)	— — ••
I I-vy	••	R Re-becc-a	• — •		

As you can see, the word picked for each letter of the alphabet begins with that same letter (except for two). And each word has as many syllables as each code letter has dots and dashes. The long syllables in each word are dashes; the short syllables are dots.

When you've memorized these twenty-six words, you've also memorized the Morse Code.

Invisible Ink

■ Lemon juice makes an excellent invisible ink. Cut a lemon in half and squeeze the juice into a small dish. Use anything that has a point—a dried up pen, the wrong end of a match, etc. Dip the point into the "ink," but don't use too much, or else the paper will wrinkle. Printing is usually easier to read than cursive.

■ To make the message visible, hold the paper up to a warm lightbulb for 10 or 15 seconds.

■ Milk can also be used for invisible ink.

■ Another good idea is to write your message between the lines of an already-written letter. The hidden message will turn up when the paper's exposed to heat, and the original letter or note will serve as a decoy.

Collecting

There's almost nothing that people won't collect—glass eyes, string, barbed wire—you name it and someone probably has a house full of it. Museum basements all over the world are jammed with people's collections. It would take another book to make a complete list, but here's a collection (in no particular order) of *just a few* of the things that kids like to collect:

Rocks, seashells, seaglass, butterflies, acorns, leaves, coins, stamps, rubber stamps, postcards, playing cards, baseball cards, stuffed animals, glass animals, comic books, heart-shaped boxes, Pez dispensers, candles, keychains, keys, cat figurines, dog figurines, any-animal figurines, pens, pencils, pencils with town names on them, erasers, girlfriends, yarn-loop-chains, business cards, toothbrushes, G.I. Joes, bugs, pictures of snakes, pictures of white tigers, pictures of horses, anything to do with horses, hair, rings, candy wrappers, cans, buttons—and that's just for starters!

TWO UNUSUAL THINGS TO COLLECT

A Spider Web: Find an abandoned spider web. Spray the web with hair spray. Press a sheet of black construction paper on the web. The web will stick to the paper.

A Twig Alphabet: Twigs grow in all kinds of shapes. Find ones that form letters. Y's and V's are easy to spot, but if you look closer, you'll find other letters. You can combine several twigs to make tricky letters like Q or R. Glue your twig alphabet to a large piece of posterboard and mount it on a wall.

Make a Rainbow

Try this on a sunny day.

If your mother will let you borrow her diamond ring for just a few minutes, try rotating it in the sun to make an instant rainbow.

If she says "no" to the ring idea, try this one:

Find a table that's directly in the sun. Fill a glass of water almost to the top. Carefully put it on the edge of a table so that it is half off the table. Put a sheet of blank, white paper on the floor beneath the glass. Keep fiddling with the paper and glass until you get the angle right for a rainbow.

WHAT MAKES A RAINBOW?

Although sunlight looks white or yellow, it's really red, orange, yellow, green, blue, indigo, and violet all mixed together. A rainbow is simply white light that has been bent in different angles by raindrops. The drops of water separate the colors.

A prism, such as the diamond ring, bends light, turning ordinary daylight into a rainbow of color. To see a rainbow outdoors, you have to have both rain and sunshine.

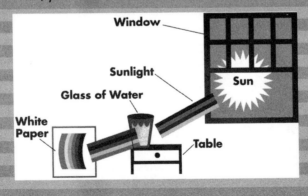

Window

Sunlight

Sun

Glass of Water

White Paper

Table

8.

Things TO DO Outside

To most boys, the world is divided into two halves—inside and outside. Inside is where it's warm and quiet. Outside is where almost *anything* can happen, from football to kick-the-can.

Sports & Games

Touch Football

Here are three touch-football plays designed by Bear Bryant, a famous coach for Alabama's Crimson Tide. For these plays, you'll need six boys to a team.

For this first play, the left end, right end, and right fullback run deep patterns and the center drops back to block. The left halfback breaks to his right and takes a lateral pass from the quarterback. After throwing the ball, the quarterback runs left, gets a return pass from the left halfback, and looks downfield for an open receiver. The right halfback is his primary receiver.

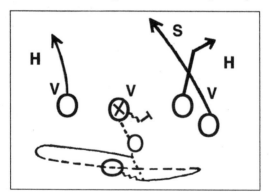

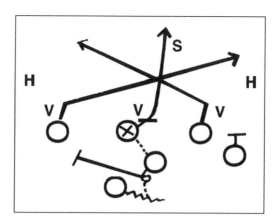

Everybody's moving on this second play. The ends cross in midfield, and the center runs up the middle. Meanwhile, the quarterback throws a lateral pass to his fullback, who looks around, finds the most open person, and throws.

For the third play, below, the quarterback receives the hike a few yards deep and everyone else runs a pass pattern. The quarterback, who has no protection, looks downfield, and quickly throws to an unguarded receiver.

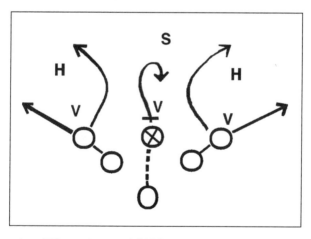

To get an NFL catalog send $1.00 to:

Team NFL Catalog
10812 Alder Circle, Suite 1529
Dallas, TX 75238

What the Ref's Signals Mean

Touchdown   **Interference**   **Illegal Procedure**

Holding   **Time Out**   **First Down**

Baseball

How to Throw a Baseball
The hardest thing to remember about throwing is that you throw with your whole body, including your arm and shoulder, not just with your arm and wrist.

■ Extend your arm far backward. Don't bend your arms sharply at the elbow. The elbow should be behind you, not sticking out in front.

■ As you bring your arm high over your head, begin striding forward with the opposite foot.

■ As your arm comes forward in a whiplike motion, the other foot comes forward. Immediately after the ball is released, your feet should be parallel again.

How to Read a Baseball Boxscore

Boxscores are found at the end of newspaper stories about ball games.

The letters after a player's name tell what position he plays:

c: Catcher

p: Pitcher

1b: First base

2b: Second base

3b: Third base

ss: Shortstop

lf: Left field

cf: Center field

rf: Right field

ph: Pinch hitter

Here's what the letters above each column mean:

ANGELS 8, ROYALS 5

KANSAS CITY	AB	R	H	BI	BB	SO	Avg.
Halter cf	3	0	2	0	0	0	.290
Offerman ph-2b	2	1	2	0	0	0	.305
J. Hansen 2b	2	0	1	0	1	1	.282
Damon ph-cf	2	0	0	0	0	1	.282
J. Bell ss	3	0	0	0	0	3	.290
C. Davis dh	4	0	0	0	0	2	.291
J. King 1b	4	1	1	1	0	1	.229
Palmer 3b	4	2	2	1	0	0	.258
Dye rf	4	0	0	0	0	3	.231
Y. Benitez lf	2	1	1	2	1	1	.273
RD Myers ph	1	0	0	0	0	0	.306
Mi. Sweeney c	3	0	0	0	0	1	.243
Cooper ph	1	0	0	0	0	0	.210
Totals	35	5	9	5	2	14	–
ANAHEIM	AB	R	H	BI	BB	SO	Avg.
Henderson lf	4	1	0	1	1	0	.200
Phillips dh	3	2	1	0	1	0	.282
Salmon rf	3	1	0	0	1	1	.296
Hollins 3b	3	1	1	1	1	2	.283
Eenhoorn 3b	0	0	0	0	0	0	..
Edmonds cf	3	0	0	1	1	1	.284
Turner 1b	2	0	0	0	0	2	.333
Erstad ph-1b	2	0	1	2	0	0	.301
Alicea 2b	3	2	1	0	1	0	.253
Kreuter c	4	1	1	2	0	1	.222
DiSarcina ss	4	0	1	0	0	0	.240
Totals	31	8	6	7	6	7	–

Kansas City	010	300	100–5	9	2
Anaheim	220	100	30x–8	6	1

AB: The number of times each player was at bat during the game. It does not count as an at-bat if a player walks, is hit by a pitched ball, or makes a sacrifice hit.

R: The number of times the player has made it safely across home plate—that is, the number of times he's made runs.

H: The number of times a player got a hit—that is, hit the ball so he got on base safely. It doesn't count as a hit if a player gets on base because the other team made an error.

RBI: Runs batted in; whenever a batter brings another player home, he usually gets an RBI.

E: Errors

DP: Double plays

LOB: Left on base

SB: Stolen bases

CS: Caught stealing

You'll find these letters next to the pitcher's stats:

IP: The number of innings a pitcher pitches.

H: The number of hits a pitcher gives up.

R: The number of runs that score.

ER: The number of earned runs—that is, the runs that are used to compile the pitcher's *ERA*, or earned run average. (The lower the ERA, the better.)

BB: Bases on balls. The number of times a pitcher whaled a batter.

SO: Strike outs.

W: The number of wins the pitcher has.

S: The number of saves the pitcher has.

At the bottom of the pitcher's line stats, you'll sometimes see these letters:

WP: Wild pitch

PB: Passed ball—that is, the ball was gotten by the catcher.

How to Throw a Fast Ball

Fastballs are fun to throw, because—well, because they go *fast*.

It's even more fun when you can throw them where you want them to go. You can strike out a lot of batters that way. A good fast ball will hop up toward the batter as it nears the end of its flight.

Drag Finger Tips On Upper Surface

Hold the ball with your fingers pressed firmly against the seams, thumb on the bottom.

When you throw the ball, the two upper fingers will leave the ball later than the thumb, since they are far-ther forward. This creates what's called *drag* on the surface of the ball, which is what causes the ball to spin and rotate. If you throw this pitch fast enough, you'll get a hop on the ball.

WHAT MAKES A BALL CURVE?

As a fast-pitched ball plows through the air, it's also spinning around on itself. The spin is what causes the ball to curve, or "break." At the beginning of a pitch, the force of the throw is stronger than the force of the spin, so the spin doesn't have much effect. (This is why a ball doesn't break as soon as it's thrown.) Toward the end of the pitch, the force of the throw is weaker, and the spin takes effect.

Since a ball always curves in the direction it's spinning, to control the curve you have to control the spin. A lot easier said than done, of course. But try getting started with a Whiffle ball.

How to Find the "Sweet Spot" on Your Bat

Hang a baseball on a piece of string from the edge of a porch or table. Hold your bat with your thumb and middle finger so the bat hangs down and swings, using your fingers as a pivot point. Let the bat swing gently against the dangling baseball. Not hard, though. When you find the spot where the bat doesn't vibrate at all when it hits the ball, you've found the sweet spot. It's usually about three to six inches from the fat end of the bat. In a game, if you hit the ball on this spot, it'll really travel.

Swipe-a-Dozen

Not only a lot of fun, this game also helps you perfect your base-stealing and rundown skills.

For safety, it's probably best to use a rubber ball, instead of a real baseball.

Two bases are set 30' apart, with a fielder guarding each. The runners position themselves on one or the other of the bases. As the fielders begin tossing the ball back and forth, the runners try to "steal" the other base without being tagged out.

The object is to swipe twelve bases without being tagged out six times. (The numbers may vary, depending on skill level.) As in baseball, an out is also declared if a runner leaves the baseline.

The Infield Fly Rule Explained

The point of this rule is to keep the defensive team from making a double play by deliberately dropping an easy pop to force out a base runner.

Here's how it works: With runners on first and second base and fewer than two outs, a batter who hits an easy pop to the infield is automatically out. The runners may proceed at their own risk—but, generally, they do so only if they're stupid.

Three Balls You Can Make Yourself

Superball To make a superball, all you need is a crumpled piece of paper and lots and lots of rubber bands. You can buy a box of rubber bands at a stationery store, or you can collect them from friends and family. Crumple up a piece of paper, and then twist a rubber band around it. Keep going until you run out of rubber bands, or time. When you bounce your superball, rubber bands will go shooting off it in all directions!

Indoor Tailball Take an old pair of tights or stockings and cut off one of the legs halfway down. Stuff the rest of the tights into the toe of the cut-off leg. Twist the toe, then turn the leg inside-out, so that all the material is contained in the toe. Tie knots at the toe and the end of the tailball. Throw it like a sling. It goes very fast.

Outdoor Tailball Same as above, but instead of stuffing the leg with the rest of the stocking, put a tennis ball or a superball in the leg. Tie and throw.

HERE'S AN INDOOR BALL YOU CAN MAKE

Take a roll of 3/4" masking tape and wrap it around a piece of crumpled paper. Keep wrapping until your ball is the size you want.

Bike Rally

Everyone in the neighborhood can join in the rally.

Make sure everyone wears helmets!

Decorate your bikes with streamers and flags. Pick a length of road for the rally course. End the rally with a big cookout.

"In our bike rally we had a lead car (which was also decorated) that played *The 1812 Overture*," says one kid.

Your Personal Olympics

To hold your own Olympics, you need to come up with five or ten events.

You might have a high jump, a long jump, hurdles, a throw for accuracy (throwing a ball through a tire), a distance throw, a bicycle race—anything you can think of. Of course, you'll need a running event!

You'll need timers and tape measures.

When you set up your events make sure there's enough room to throw or run without hitting each other or a neighbor, and check that long jumpers have a soft place to land.

Record the first-, second-, and third-place winners. Keep track of the scores. First place: 5 points; second place: 3 points; third place: 1 point.

You can award medals for each event or for the three top overall scores.

How to Make Gold, Silver, and Bronze Medals

You'll need plaster of paris (available at any hobby store); a plastic yogurt container's lid, and straw for each medal you make; and silver, gold, and bronze spray or model paint.

Mix up the plaster of paris according to the directions on the package, and pour a little bit—about ¼"—in each yogurt lid. (Some kinds of yogurt have a top that is just about the right depth.) Stick your straw near the edge of the lid; you're making a hole to put the ribbon through.

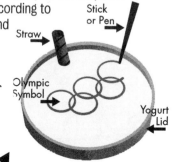

Straw · Stick or Pen · Olympic Symbol · Yogurt Lid

You might want to cut the straws into smaller pieces, so they don't topple over. Before the plaster dries completely, use a marker top, or something about that size, to impress the five Olympic rings on your medal. Or you can draw the rings with a small stick or an old pen.

When the plaster of paris dries, peel the yogurt lid away and push the straw out—you should have a hole near the top now.

Spray or paint each medal gold, silver, or bronze. Put a ribbon through the hole and you have your own Olympic-style medals!

Backyard Obstacle Course

This is pretty good fun for two to 20 kids. If you're raising money for your school or church, you can charge 50¢ for each kid to go through the course. Have someone time how long it takes each kid to run the course, and give a prize to the fastest.

Every obstacle course is different, because every backyard is different. You'll need to take advantage of your yard's special features. Here are some ideas for obstacles you can set up:

Obstacle 1: Island Hopping Round up as many large buckets as you can and have the runner step in each one, without tipping any over. If a bucket tips, make the runner start again.

Obstacle 2: Mountain Climbing Set up a series of sawhorses, ladders, or benches for the runner to climb over.

Obstacle 3: Swinging Through the Jungle If you have a tree in your yard, tie a rope swing to it. Have the runner swing out and land in a designated area (an old throw rug, for instance). If you don't have a tree, set up a broad jump.

Obstacle 4: Mystery Caves Get some large corrugated boxes—the kind appliances come in—and connect them together with gaffer's tape. Put in some dead ends, if you can. Attach some fringed material (like car-washes have) for the runner to pass through.

Obstacle 5: Crossing Piranha River Find a long ladder, and set it flat on the ground. The runner must step on each rung, without slipping. If one foot slips off, the piranhas get it, and the runner becomes a hopper. (If both feet slip, he's out.)

Obstacle 6: Whirlpool Coil some low garden fencing (or strips of corrugated box material) into a whirlpool shape. Make it just wide enough for one foot to step through at a time. If the fence tips over, the runner must go through whirlpool again.

Obstacle 7: Army ant stamp Take some bubble wrap (large bubbles are best) and cut it into even-sized pieces. Cut one piece for each runner. Have the runner pop every bubble in his sheet, before he can proceed to the next obstacle.

Obstacle 8: Under the Falls Have someone hold a garden hose with the nozzle held up, so there's a narrow arch for the runner to pass through.

Acrobatics

Try making pyramids with two other friends. Then put on some good, spangly costumes, give yourselves a snappy name—"The Amazing Rollinos," for example—and put on a show for your parents or friends.

Pool Games

Here are some fun things to try when you're in a swimming pool. If you're at a public pool, remember to check first if games and diving are allowed. And never swim without a lifeguard!

Marco Polo

The object of the game is for the person who's It to catch other players while his eyes are shut tightly. It goes to the middle of the pool and everyone else swims around him. He tries to find the other swimmers by calling out, "Marco!" When he does this, everyone else has to shout out "Polo!" which gives away their locations. Once a player is caught, he becomes It.

HOW TO GET AWAY FAST UNDERWATER

Make this dive when you're already swimming in the water. It's called a "pike dive" and it's good for getting out of the way fast in games like Marco Polo.

Before you start your dive, take a deep breath. Bend sharply at your waist into a V position. Your hips will rise out of the water.

As you begin to sink, stick your legs straight up. The momentum will push you down into the water. As soon as your feet get underwater, start to flutter-kick.

How to Make a Feet-First Surface Dive

This is a dive you make when you're already in the water.

Standing straight up in the water, as though you're treading water, give a good, strong scissors kick. While kicking, push your hands down hard to your sides.

The momentum will send you rising out of the water. Now, as you start back down, bring both hands up until your head is underwater. Next, use a breaststroke to bring yourself into swimming position and go!

Water Dodgeball

Use a rubber ball. One team makes a ring around the other team's players. The players inside the circle can duck or dive underwater—do everything they can to avoid being hit, but leave the circle. The players on the outside ring try to hit the players on the inside—just like regular dodgeball. Once a player is hit he joins the outside circle.

Variation: Just one player is in the middle—everyone else is outside. The middle player can dive, duck, or swim underwater to keep from being hit. As above, though, he can't leave the circle. The player who hits him with the ball takes his place.

Backyard Games

Shark Attack

Another tag game. One person is the shark and he tries to "attack" (tag) the "swimmers" (everyone else). Shark territory is the slide and asphalt is the "ocean." Swings are "beach" (safe) territory. For the game to be really fun, there should be more swimmers than swings.

The shark sits on top of the slide, while the swimmers get closer and closer to him. When he slides down, everyone yells "Shark attack!" If the shark tags a swimmer, he brings him back to the place under the slide. Other swimmers try to free their fellow swimmers.

Mother, May I?

Put two lengths of brightly-colored yarn on opposite ends of the yard, making a "start" and a "finish" line. One boy (the caller) stands behind the finish line, and the rest of the group (the runners) stand behind the start line. The caller chooses a runner by name, saying "Bob, take two giant steps forward." Bob then says, "Mother, may I?" to which the caller can either say "Yes," or change his mind and say, "No. Take two scissor steps instead." (Or baby steps, hops, backwards steps, forward rolls, or anything else he can think of.) Bob then takes the required steps. The caller continues down the line of runners, asking for various steps. He can mix the steps up (one giant step forward, two baby steps back, for instance) but each runner must move forward, each time—even if it's just a tiny bit. If a player forgets to say, "Mother, may I?" he has to go back to the beginning. The first player to cross the finish line becomes the next caller.

Red Light, Green Light

This game is set up the same way as "Mother, May I." The caller yells, "Green light!" and turns his back to the runners, who run forward as fast as they can. After a few seconds, the caller yells, "Red light!" and spins around. If any of the runners is still in motion, he must return to the start line. The first runner to cross the finish line becomes the next caller.

Red Rover

Divide the group into two teams, with both teams facing each other about fifty paces apart. The players on each team link arms. In Red Rover, each player gets a chance to be a caller, in turn. (You can start at one end of the line and move down towards the other end.) The first caller yells to the other team, "Red rover, red rover, let Richard come over." Richard breaks away from his line, and charges toward the opposite team's line. If he's able to break through it, he gets to return to his own team. If not, he must join the opposite team. The game continues until all the boys are on one team (or everyone gets bored with the game).

Prison

A very old favorite, this playground game has a zillion variations.

■ **Pick boundaries** for your playing field—a bench, a fence, a sandbox—anything you choose, and decide on a jail area.

■ **To start, players divide into teams.** The players on one team all hide first, while the other team hides its eyes and counts to 50. Players must hide within the designated area.

■ **When a searcher finds one** of the opposing players, he has to hold on to him long enough to slowly count three (one, one thousand; two, one thousand; three, one thousand—like that). Then the enemy is a prisoner and has to go to jail.

■ **One member of the searching team** guards the jail. But if a free teammate runs through the jail, all of the prisoners get to escape. Then the prisoners get to run and hide again.

■ **When everyone on the hiding team** is finally caught and in jail, the other team gets to hide and the game begins all over again.

Bowling

The basic four-step delivery.

Step One
■ **Stand at the Foul Line.** Turn your back to the pins and take four steps away from the foul line. Add a half step for your slide. Now turn around and face the pins. Take a couple of practice walks to make sure you're four steps and a slide away from the foul line. You're aiming for the diamond, or dot, that's to the right (if you're right handed) of the center dot.

■ **Stance.** The stance is your starting position. Most of the weight of the ball should be on your non-bowling hand. Hold the ball anywhere from your waist to your shoulders. Keep your arm close to your body and your eyes on the target. Your toes should be straight and your knees slightly flexed.

■ **The Pushaway.** This is the first step of your approach. Push the ball forward as you take a step. Try to keep your movements smooth—not jerky.

Step Two
■ **Begin Your Backswing.** Bring the ball down and begin your backswing. Make sure your arm is close to your body. You're getting near the line, but don't get nervous!

Step Three
■ **Bring the Ball Back to Its Furthest Point.** At the end of this step, the ball should be at the top of its backswing.

Step Four
■ **Slide and Release** The fourth step should be a slide. Your arm should smoothly ease the ball over the foul line.

■ **Follow Through** After the ball is released, your arm should continue the swing that started right in the beginning. Your arm should be pointed toward the target.

CLOTHESPIN BOWLING

You'll need about twenty wooden clothespins. Pin two clothespins together at an angle to make them stand up. Set the pins in place and, using a tennis ball, knock them down as you would real pins, at a real alley.

Small frozen orange juice containers also make good pins. After washing them out, put about a half inch of plaster of paris in the bottom and proceed as above.

To cheat, substitute heavier "pins"—with, say, an inch of plaster of paris—when it's your opponent's turn.

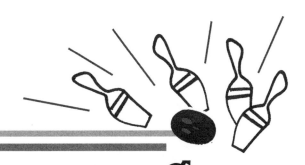

Darkball

You will need:

- A dark yard or room
- A dark-colored Koosh or Nerf ball
- Two or more players

The object of the game is simple: Hit the players on the other team with the ball. Every hit is a point. If an opposing player catches the ball, he gets the point. The tough part is it all takes place in the dark.

It's sometimes necessary to turn the lights on or use a flashlight to find a ball. This counts as a "time out." Each team gets only four time outs—after that it's a penalty, which means they have to give the ball back to the other team.

Note: There's a fair amount of trust required in Darkball. if you're not going to admit when you're hit, the game'll fall apart pretty fast.

Kick the Can

You put a tin can in the middle of a little circle about a yard across. One boy is It. One of the other kids kicks the can as hard as he can kick it, and the boy who is It has to count to ten slowly, then go get the can and put it back into the circle. Meanwhile, everybody else runs and hides. The kid who is It has to try to find one of the other kids. As soon as he sees a boy who is hiding, he has to yell, "I see you!" and the name of the kid he sees. Then they both race to the can. Whoever gets there first immediately kicks the can again. The kid who gets there second has to go and get the can (but this time, he doesn't have to count to ten), put it in the circle, and go look for the kids who are still hiding.

Follow the Leader

This one dates back hundreds of years, but it's amazing how many kids have never played it. By the way, as always, the more, the merrier.

Nothing could be simpler. Everyone follows after the leader, doing exactly what he does, going wherever he goes. Over walls, up trees, down alleys, through tunnels.

You don't have to be a great athlete to be a good leader, but you should have a good imagination. The best games of follow the leader have both easy and hard stunts. As a leader you can also do funny walks, somersaults, or slither like a snake—virtually anything you dream up.

Bouncing Bombs

You'll need three pots and three tennis balls. Place the pots in a row several feet apart. Then make a line about 10' from the first pot. Standing behind the line, you must try to bounce the balls into the pots on ONE bounce. More than that and the throw doesn't count.

Each player gets three bounce-tosses per turn. (That's why there are three balls—unless you want to spend all your time chasing balls around the room.)

If the ball lands in the closest pot, one point. If it lands in the second pot, three points. The third pot is worth five big points. And if a player gets all three balls into pots in one turn, he gets a bonus of ten!

The first one to score 50 points wins. *Don't forget:* one bounce only!

Flourball War!

Flourballs make great ammo. Stockpile an arsenal, and let 'er rip! You'll need:

- Flour—as much as you can get your hands on
- A box of facial tissues
- Twist ties—one for each tissue

To make a flourball, cup a Kleenex in your hand and put in some flour. Gather the tissue at the top and secure the flourball with a twist-tie. (You may want to cut your twist-ties in half, to make them last longer. You can always recycle twist-ties from already-deployed flourballs.)

Instead of water balloons, put water in a plastic sandwich bag and use a twist-tie to close it. With 100 baggies costing about a dollar, you'll get a lot more bang for your buck.

Make a Catapult

You'll need a ruler, a block of wood, a plastic spoon, some strong tape, and a bag of mini-marshmallows. Put the ruler on the wood block and tape it in place. Tape the plastic spoon to the opposite side. Put a marshmallow in the spoon. Hold the catapult in place by putting your knee on the ruler. Bend back the spoon, and launch the marshmallow. Make a target, and see how good you are at hitting it with your ammo.

Marshmallow
Plastic Spoon
Tape
Ruler
Wood Block

Plastic Army Wars

You'll need at least thirty plastic soldiers and one marble. Play this one on concrete or on an uncarpeted floor; alone or in teams.

■ Divide a bunch of army men into two equal groups.

■ Set up your men about 20 inches apart, deploying soldiers in any formation you choose.

■ Roll your marble into the opposite battalion, trying to knock down men.

The first side to have all the soldiers "die" loses.

Two Amazing Feats of Strength

■ **The Human Airplane:** You'll need one person to be the airplane and three people to carry it. The airplane lies face-down, with both arms spread out like wings. One person holds his right arm, while another person holds his left arm. A third person holds both legs. He tries to stay as rigid as he can while he is picked up and slowly carried around. (He only needs to be a few feet off the ground.) When he can't hold the position any-more, he cries, "Crashing!" and his carriers *carefully* set him down.

■ **The Human Bridge:** To make a human bridge you'll need at least five kids. The more kids you have, the longer your bridge will be. Two rows of kids face each other. Each boy holds both arms of the boy he's facing. The arms need to be tightly gripped, right below the elbows. Another kid (the lightest one) begins to walk barefoot across the "rungs" of the bridge. (The walker can use a chair or stepstool to climb onto the human bridge.) As the walker steps from one rung to the next, the two boys who have made the rung he's stepped off of run to the head of the line, join arms, and extend the bridge. The game continues until the walker stumbles, or the bridge gets tired.

After-Rain Races

After there's been a good rain, look for a gutter or stream with a nice, strong current. Use leaves or different-colored toothpicks for your boats—anything that skims over the water quickly. Drop your crafts in the water and race down to the end of the course to see which boat wins. You can build obstacles with gravel and dirt, and make a dam at the end of the course.

An Acorn Cap Racer

Leaf
Mud   Acorn Cap

A Walnut Shell Cruiser

Leaf
Walnut Shell   Mud

Beachcombing

The best time to go beachcombing is when the tide is low. That's when you can collect all kinds of treasures the high tide has left behind, like shells, seaweed, crabs, jellyfish, driftwood, sea glass—sometimes even jewelry and money!

There are two high and two low tides every twenty-four hours, but their times vary from one day to the next. Check the local paper to find out the times of the high and low tides.

High and low tides are caused by the gravitational force of the moon. The moon pulls the water away from Earth, the way a distant magnet pulls on metal filings. The part of Earth that is closest to the moon will experience a high tide. On the opposite side of the world, there will also be a high tide, but for a different reason: because the force of the spinning earth is pushing water away from its surface. When tides are highest in one part of the world, they are lowest in another.

The absolutely best time to go beachcombing is right after (not during!) a storm. When the ocean gets churned up, all kinds of neat stuff is thrown onto the shore.

"SPRING" AND "NEAP" TIDES

Once every month, the tide is especially high. This is because there is an extra force pulling on Earth's water: the sun. When the sun, moon, and Earth are lined up, the gravitational pull is increased and more water is pulled away from Earth. These extra-high tides are called "spring" tides. Because the high tides are higher, the low tides become even lower during this period.

A spring tide is a great time to go beachcombing.

When the sun and the moon are at a 45° angle to Earth, the moon's gravitational pull is at its weakest. The difference between high and low tides is less pronounced during this period. This phenomenon is called a "neap" tide.

BEACHCOMBER'S LAMP

A t any large hobby shop or lighting store, you can buy a "bottle assembly kit." These kits cost around $7 and include all of the stuff (cork, wire, plug, and socket) you'll need to turn a bottle into a lamp. Collect enough small shells and seaglass to fill a clear wine bottle. Follow directions on the kit.

Beach Art

- Always work with damp sand.

- Plasterer's putty knives and wallpaper brushes make great shaping and smoothing tools.

- When making sand animals, you're better off working from a picture than from memory.

Make a Drip Castle
Fill a large bucket halfway with sand, then fill it the rest of the way with water. Grab a handful of the wet sand and let it drip onto the area where you want your castle to be.

Sending Beach Messages to Low-Flying Aircraft
Write a message in letters big enough (think HUGE) to be seen from way up high.

HI UP THERE!
FEEL FREE TO
SEND DOWN
SOME SNACKS

Outdoor Creations

Stilts

Wood Stilts

You'll need two pieces of wood, each about 2" wide, 1" thick, and 2' longer than you are.

Use two pieces of board for foot rests. Cut the foot rests at a slight angle into two equal shapes, as shown in the picture. The higher you put the footrests, the taller you'll be.

Attach the foot rests to the stilts with three screws.

Tin Can Stilts

Large juice cans work especially well. Using a hammer and nail, punch two holes in each can on opposite sides about an inch down.

Now string some sturdy cord (the length depends on how tall you are) through the holes and up to waist height, tying the two ends together with a strong finishing knot. Repeat the procedure for the other can and you're ready to do some can stilt-walking.

STiLT JousTiNG

You're the knight. The stilts are your horse. The cardboard tubes that come with wrapping paper are your lances!

The Object: Use your lance to knock your opponent off his stilt-horse.

A Clock Putting Green

You don't need acres and acres of fairway to work on your golf game. All you need is your lawn, a sharp stick, a piece of string, twelve golf tees, and a tin cup. Let your folks know what you're up to, because you'll be digging a hole in the middle of your homemade golf course.

■ **First, ask an adult to mow the lawn as closely as possible for you.** (You might want to offer to rake the lawn first to soften up the adult.) Estimate where the middle of your lawn is, and put the wooden stick in that spot. Next, take a 24' piece of string, and mark its middle (at 12'). Tie the string to the stake in the middle. Think of the circle that the string makes, as it sweeps around the stake, as a big clock.

■ **Find 12:00 and mark it with a tee.** Make a straight line to the opposite side, and mark 6:00 with another tee. Next, mark 3:00 and 9:00 the same way. Fill in the other "hours" with tees, until you have a circle that is divided into twelve even sections. Remove the stake and dig a hole at the center spot. Put a small tin cup in the hole. (The top of the cup should be at ground level.) Now that your golf course is set up, you're ready to play.

■ **Starting at 1:00,** try to hit the ball into the can in two shots (*par*). If you do, move on to 2:00. Your entire course will be par 24. See how close you can get to par, as you travel around the clock. If you're playing with others, proceed as above. If you fail to get the ball into each cup in two tries, though, let the second player take his turn. Continue in this fashion, until all of you have hit "around the clock." If you want to get fancy, you can create some obstacles, and make some shots harder than others.

GOLF COURSE BUSINESSES

If you live near a golf course, you can always make a little extra money recovering lost balls from the rough and selling them to golfers. Shine them up a little first. If they're in good shape, sell them for half the cost of a new ball. If they have dings, sell them for less. You'll be surprised how many balls you can find (and how many balls the golfers lose!). If it's okay with the golf course, sell lemonade and iced tea near the ninth hole. Golfers get pretty thirsty halfway through the course and usually welcome some refreshment. Cookies and brownies are good sellers, too.

A Rope Ladder

All you need to make a rope ladder is two lengths of sturdy rope, some cord, and some notched wood, for rungs.

1. Decide where your ladder is going to go, then get enough rope for twice the length it will cover, plus some extra for hanging and knots. The rope should be the kind that has strands that can be twisted apart.

2. Cut ten 12" rungs from 1' x 1' board. If your ladder is going to be an especially long one, you'll need more rungs.

3. Now your whittling skills are going to come in handy; make notches on both ends of each rung. Notch all four edges.

4. Tie the two ropes together, leaving some extra rope on top.

5. Tie a knot on each rope 18" down from the top knot.

6. Separate the rope right above the knot and slide a rung through one, then the other, rope.

7. Lash the rungs to the rope with cord.

8. Go down another foot, and tie two more knots. Repeat steps 6 and 7, until you've run out of rope.

9. Tie the end of each rope, so it won't unravel.

Make sure you hang your rope ladder from a branch strong enough to support some weight.

Vine Fort

This will take a month and half or so to grow into a real fort, so start as soon as you can.

In a sunny part of the yard or garden, make a circle of short, wooden stakes. Put the stakes about a foot apart, except for the "doorway," which should have a couple of feet between stakes.

Pound a very tall pole or stake in the middle of the circle. String twine from each stake to the top of the pole. At this point, your "fort" will look like a string teepee.

Now plant pole beans at the bottom of each wooden stake. As the beans start to grow, wind them around the string. By the time the beans reach the top of the pole, you'll have a terrific fort. Don't forget to water your fort!

Branch Lean-To Fort

You'll need a tree with a fork, a long branch or pole, and lots of shorter branches and sticks.

Stick the long branch in the fork of the tree, so that you have a triangle shape.

Now take your shorter branches and lean them against the main pole. Cross-hatch the branches or sticks so that you'll have a frame-work for lacing in more branches for maximum coverage and camouflage. Do it on both sides.

Leave room for a door!

Rock Sculptures

Use rocks and other found materials to make your own outdoor sculptures. The tricky part is getting the arrangement to balance.

Backyard Sundial

Find a pole about 2" wide and 4' long. You may have to go to a lumberyard. Sharpen one end and stick the pole in the ground in a sunny spot. Next, nail a smooth board, about 8" square, onto the top of the pole. Using a good strong glue, attach a wooden chopstick upright at the center of the board. A knitting needle will also work very well—hammer it gently into place.

When the sun is out and shining, you can begin marking your clock. Start in the morning. Using a watch or clock, see where the needle or chopstick or whatever you use casts its shadow at 9 A.M. Make a mark where the shadow ends, and write the number 9—or IX, if you're using Roman numerals. (See the chart, below.) Do this every hour, as long as there's enough sun for the chopstick or needle to cast a shadow.

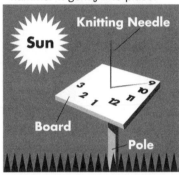

A Few Common Sundial Inscriptions

- Time and tide tarry for no man.
- *Tempus fugit.* (Time flies.)
- *Sic transit gloria mundi.* (Thus passes the glory of the world.)

CLOCK NUMERALS

Sometimes, clocks use Roman numerals for figures. Here's how to translate the Roman numerals into modern numbers, and vice-versa:

I	II	III	IV	V	VI	VII	VIII	IX	X	XI	XII
1	2	3	4	5	6	7	8	9	10	11	12

Let It Snow!

Snowman Building Tips

■ The bottom ball is twice as wide as the middle ball, and the middle ball is twice as wide as the top ball.

■ Pour water over your snowman before you go to bed so it will have a coating of ice and stay around longer. (You can also firm up snow balls by keeping them in the freezer overnight.)

Snow Fort

Snow forts are great because they give you a place to hide and they also help defend you against snowball attacks.

Make of bunch of great big snow balls and roll them over to your building area. Arrange the first layer of snow balls in a circle, leaving room for a door. Now you're ready

to add the next layer of snow balls. Don't put the snow balls right on top of each other—stagger them, the way a bricklayer does when building a wall.

Keep layering the snowballs until your fort is as tall as you like. You can make windows by leaving a space, then putting a board over the top to continue stacking the snowballs.

Use branches or plywood boards for the roof. Crisscrossed pine boughs work very nicely. Pile snow on top of the boards or branches to hold them down. Make sure all your boards are strong enough to sup-

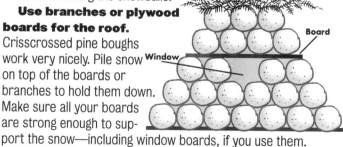

Pine Branches

Board

Window

port the snow—including window boards, if you use them.

Floor Plan for a Real Igloo

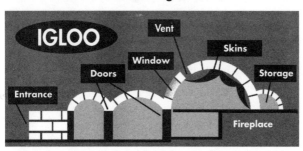

Animal Tracks to Look for in the Snow

Cat

Rat   Mouse

Skunk   Squirrel   Woodchuck   Raccoon

Maple Syrup Ice Cream

There isn't any cream in this, but it tastes like ice cream! Pour some maple syrup on a thick layer of freshly fallen snow. The syrup will freeze and turn solid. Pick up the syrup and eat it quickly, before it melts.

Backyard Skating Rink

I f you have freezing, or below, temperatures and a level back-yard, this is easy and fun. Later in the day, toward evening, is the best time to make your rink.

Shovel all the snow in the backyard against the fence to make sides for the rink. Get a garden hose, adjust the nozzle to make a fine spray, then spray the shoveled area with water.

The trick is to make thin layers of ice, one layer at a time. Don't make puddles. Work methodically, across and back again, to make each layer. Be patient—it's worth it.

Camping & Campcraft

How to Pitch a Tent

■ First, practice indoors. Invite your friends over for an indoor camp-out. The more familiar you are with how to pitch your tent, the easier it will be when you have to do it outside in the wilderness.

■ Find the right location. Your tent site should be on a level surface, with plenty of clear space around all sides of the tent.

■ Watch for water. Don't pitch your tent right next to a stream bed or where run-off will flood you if it should start to rain.

■ Keep the floor dry. Most tents come with a built-in ground cover. If yours doesn't, make sure to use one.

Useful Knots

The very best way to learn to tie a knot is probably to join the Boy Scouts. The next, is to have a Boy Scout show you. Other-wise, study these pictures and practice, practice, practice!

■ **Over Hand:** A finishing knot

- **Square Knot:** A good knot for tying two strings or ropes together

- **Clove Hitch:** A good knot for lashing or tying ropes to posts

- **Two Half Hitches:** Also good for tying things to posts (a horse to a hitching post, for example)

Nature Scavenger Hunt

This is a variation on a standard scavenger hunt—except all the items to be found are natural, not man-made. For example, you could have the players find a piece of quartz, a bird feather, a clover leaf, a maple leaf, a wild onion (if it's spring)—a mixture of hard and easy to find objects. The list will depend on where you live and the time of year.

Hazardous Plants

Learn what these plants look like, and then avoid them!

Poison Ivy **Poison Oak** **Poison Sumac**

Trail Signs

Native Americans used trail signs to help them find their way back home or so that other Indians could follow them. Soon explorers, scouts, trappers, and hunters adopted these same Indian trail signs or developed their own. After a while, the signs became more or less standardized. Certain standard trail signs are recognized everywhere:

Branch: This Is Trail

Branch: Turn Left

Branch: Turn Right

Danger

Pebble: This Is Trail

Pebble: Turn Left

Pebble: Turn Right

Rock: This Is Trail

Rock: Turn Left

Rock: Turn Right

Sticks: This Is Trail

Sticks: Turn Left

Sticks: Turn Right

Not only is it fun to blaze a trail, you can also play games like "Hares and Hounds" using trail markers.

HoW To PLAY HARES AND HoUNDS

Half the group are hounds and the other half are hares. The hares start out about half an hour before the hounds. The hares mark their trail using trail signs. Thirty minutes later, the hounds set out after the hares, using the signs to track them down. It's a good idea for the hares to have lunch or dessert waiting for the whole group—that way the hounds have a real incentive to find them and won't give up!

Using a Compass

■ Hold the compass level and still until the needle stops moving. Always double check by gently turning the compass over a few times and then taking a new reading.

■ To get a true reading be sure to keep the compass away from metal. The blue end of the needle points to the north magnetic pole, which a few degrees off from true north.

■ Remember that compasses affect each other. Your compass won't be accurate if several other compasses are nearby. If your compass needle stops with a sudden jerk instead of coming to a quivering stop, be sure to check for metal or some other disturbance near the compass.

Finding Your Direction Without a Compass

■ **Moss generally grows thickest est on the north side of trees.** (The north side gets the least sun and stays damp longest.) But not always. Sometimes trees are shaded on the south and moss can grow on a different side, or even all around a tree. However, in a heavily wooded area, moss is usually thickest on the north or northwest.

■ **Evergreen tree needle tips,** especially hemlocks, generally curve toward the east.

■ **Goldenrod** If you find an open field of goldenrod, the blossom tips usually point east.

■ **Prickly lettuce** (*Lactuca scariola*) has leaves that grow vertically from the stem. Those leaves point south and north.

■ **If you have a watch with an hour hand** and it's standard, not daylight-saving, time, here's a neat trick: Hold your watch flat in your hand and point the hour hand right at the sun. South will be halfway between 12 on the watch and the hour hand. This only works north of the equator, though. If you're south of the equator (Australia, etc.), just reverse the directions.

■ **At night, look for the North Star.** Find the Big Dipper. The two stars that make up the outer side of its cup are the pointer stars. Draw an imaginary line through the pointer stars directly to the North Star, or Polaris. It's not a real bright star. But it's the one that you'll come to if you draw that imaginary line. The point on the horizon right below the North Star is due north. If you're having trouble finding the Big Dipper, see if you can find W-shaped Cassiopeia. Cassiopeia and the Big Dipper are the same distance from the North Star, but on opposite sides.

■ **If you're lost ...** Stay put and make noise or signals until you're found. If you have to walk to get to safety, always walk downhill. If you find a stream, follow it. Eventually, all streams lead to civilization.

Panning for Gold

■ **Using a large spoon, fill your gold pan** with dirt and gravel from a likely-looking crevice.

■ **Find a shallow spot in a stream**—you should be able to rest the pan in water, but the current should also be strong enough to carry away loose dirt and material. Stir the material with one hand and let the water carry away the lighter stuff. Keep

swishing and stirring. Very carefully clean all the rocks and pebbles, roots, etc., right over the pan (very important!), before throwing them away.

■ **You have to break everything down into smaller pieces** and keep stirring. Since gold is heavy (even heavier than lead!), it will sink to the bottom.

■ **Now you're ready to slough off.** Carefully lift the pan from the water. Tilt the pan just enough to spill off some of the water. Swish the water around gently to help the dirt and clay dissolve. Keep swishing and every once in a while tilt the pan to spill out more water. Stop when you're left with nothing but gravel and sand.

■ **Look for a dull, yellow gleam**—you might have gold flakes or small nuggets in there!

Where to Look for Gold
Many states, including those listed below, have areas in which gold has been found. Check with your local library or on the Internet for particularly promising locations. Good luck!

Oregon	California	Colorado	Pennsylvania
Idaho	Nevada	Arizona	New Mexico
South Dakota	Wyoming	Arkansas	Minnesota
Wisconsin	Washington	Alabama	Georgia
Montana	Virginia	Maine	South Carolina
North Carolina	Indiana	Utah	Vermont
New Hampshire	Tennessee	Massachusetts	

What to Pack for Summer Camp

Here's what one kid who has gone to camp every summer since he was seven packs every year:

■ 6 pairs of (mixed) denim, khaki and mesh shorts

■ 2 bathing suits

■ 7 big t-shirts

■ 2 pairs of long jeans

■ 2 long-sleeved shirts

■ 7 pairs of underpants

■ 15 pairs of socks (all the same color)

■ 6 sweatshirts

- 5 baseball caps
- 1 rain jacket
- 1 varsity jacket
- 1 pair of sneakers
- 1 pair of hiking boots
- 1 pair of rain boots
- 2 toothbrushes
- 2 hairbrushes
- Bug spray
- Sunscreen
- Shampoo
- Lots of food—the kind that keeps

9.
Animals & Plants

Dogs

I f you're a boy, you know there's only one pet that counts. It's a pooch. And the best place to find a best friend? You guessed it . . .

How to Get a Dog from the Pound

It's nice to get dogs from the pound whenever you can because there isn't enough room for all the stray dogs in town. That means that if a dog is put in the pound and nobody comes to get him, he's finished!

Dogs that you rescue from the pound are the best dogs because they are so grateful to you for saving their lives. The dogs that you read about in the paper who save babies from burning buildings and pull kids out of pools—many of those dogs are pound dogs.

To get one, have your parents take you down to the pound. Look around and see which dog you think is your dog. Pick that one. Your parents then have to fill out a form adopting the dog, and they have to pay a small fee for the shots the dog needs. Some pounds will also spay or neuter dogs, in order to keep the number of stray dogs down. Spayed and neutered dogs can't have puppies.

You should make a special place for your new dog before you bring him home. If he's going to live in the house with you, he will need to be housebroken.

How to Housebreak a Dog

To housebreak your dog, you have to watch him like a hawk. Just as soon as he gets ready to do his business, you rush in and grab him and take him outside. Choose a part of the yard that will be his dog potty. Eventually, he'll learn to go there whenever you let him out.

If you keep grabbing him whenever he's getting ready to you-know-what, he'll eventually get the idea. Some people swat dogs who make a doo in the house, but that's not a good idea. The dog doesn't know why you're hitting him. After all, when you have to go, you have to go. You can scold him, though. But it's better to be patient with a dog than to be yelling at him all the time.

Teaching Your Puppy to Shake Hands

The secret to this trick is teaching your puppy to shift his weight to the paw he's not shaking with. Usually a seated dog leans his weight equally on both his front paws. Your puppy (we'll call him "Jack") has to learn that when you say "Shake," it means "Shift your weight and stick out your paw."

Here's how you go about it:

■ Make Jack sit down. Next, lean over him, place your arm right next to the side of his head, take his paw, and say, "Shake!"

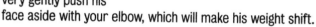

■ As you do this, very gently push his face aside with your elbow, which will make his weight shift.

■ Let go of his paw and reward him with a dog treat. Praise him: "Good boy, Jack!"

■ Repeat this exact same process four or five times. Pretty soon you'll see that Jack is beginning to shift his weight himself to avoid your elbow. At the same time, he's also lifting and sticking out his paw. After Jack starts to understand this is what you expect him to do, practice a couple of more times, then let him rest.

■ After a couple of days, you won't have to stand over him and bring your elbow near his head. He'll automatically shift his weight and extend his paw when you put your hand out and say, "Shake!"

■ Once that happens, the trick is learned. Make sure it's a habit with him by repeating it a few more times, and then stop rewarding him with a treat for doing it. Of course, you should give Jack an approving pat whenever he does the trick successfully!

■ If Jack is an older dog, he'll already know how to shift his weight. Train him the same way, leaving out the push-his-face-gently-aside-with-your-elbow part.

Horse Sense

How to Approach a Horse

You can make a bad impression on a horse, just like you can on a person. Do *not* run up to the horse and begin patting it on the nose or shoving food at it. Under no circumstances should you ever walk up *behind* a horse! Approach the horse slowly from one side while speaking its name. Get close enough for the horse to see and smell you, then slowly raise one hand and gently stroke its neck. If you've brought a treat (like an apple or carrot) hold it in your open hand and let the horse take it from you. If you treat the horse like a shy stranger, not a dumb animal, you just may make a friend for life.

How to Draw a Horse

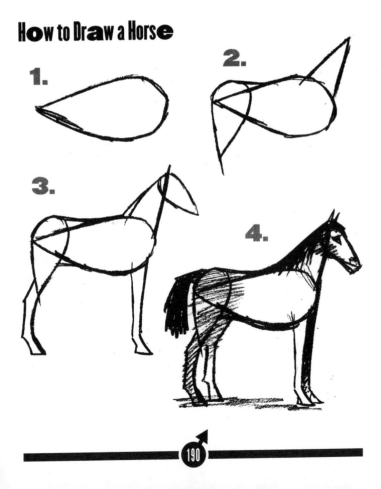

1.
2.
3.
4.

The Points of a Horse

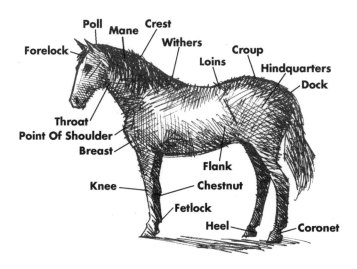

Poll Mane Crest
Forelock
Withers
Croup
Loins
Hindquarters
Dock
Throat
Point Of Shoulder
Breast
Flank
Knee
Chestnut
Fetlock
Heel
Coronet

How to Saddle a Horse

Saddling a horse is not a difficult process. There are only two variables that will affect how the job is done. One is the confidence of the boy doing the job. The other is the nervousness of the horse.

■ **Tie him.** Horses will walk away while you're saddling them unless they are restrained. Attach a lead rope to his halter and tie the rope to a post.

■ **Brush him down.** A horse's idea of fun is to roll in the dirt, and a little piece of gravel in the middle of his back can mean a big headache if you pile a saddle and a big boy on top of it.

■ **Stand on the left.** Do most of your work from the horse's left side. When horses are broken, this is part of their training. When you have to go around behind a horse, keep your hand on him as you walk, or pass far enough behind him that he won't be startled. Talk or whistle—but let him know where you are. Horses hate surprises. Unfortunately, almost anything will surprise a horse.

■ **Put on the saddle blanket.** Place the pad or blanket above the withers on the neck and slide it back into position, centered, with the front edge right at the peak of the withers.

This smoothes the hair under the blanket. If the blanket is large enough to fold, the fold should be in the front.

■ **Buckle up.** Place the saddle on the horse's back so the front edge is just above the front edge of the saddle pad. Common mistake: placing the saddle too far back. The seat belt on a saddle doesn't keep you in the seat, it keeps the seat on the horse. It's called the *cinch belt,* and it's the thing hanging down that isn't a stirrup. Working from the horse's left, reach under, grab the cinch and bring it up and through the saddle's D-ring, then back through the cinch ring, then up again to secure it. Some cinch belts tie, some buckle. How tight? Not too; just snug it in place (you'll tighten it later). There should be enough room to comfortably squeeze a couple of fingers beneath the belt, but not enough room for your whole hand. If you immediately tighten the belt, you may startle the horse.

■ **Feel for fit.** Let the animal get used to the feel of the saddle. You do the same: adjust it and make sure it feels like it's in place and secure. If the saddle has a chest band, belt it in place now.

■ **Bridle stuff:** Keep the horse restrained by placing the reins around his neck. (You can also slip the halter down until it clears his nose, then bring it back up so it forms a loop around his neck.) Holding the bit in your left hand and the headstall in your left, slide the bit into the horse's mouth and bring the headstall over his ears. If he won't say "Ah," slide a finger into the corner of his mouth; there are no choppers there, and he'll open wide for you.

■ **Ride.** Now tighten the cinch so it's secure, and mount from the left side. Show the horse you mean to control it by directing its first movements with you on its back. If you find your feet in the stirrups, but your rear end on the ground, you'll know something's amiss. Make the necessary adjustment. When the ride's over, reverse the entire process and brush down the horse. If he's hot, walk him until his breathing slows. Don't let an overheated horse drink more than a handful of water.

To learn more about horses, you can write the following organizations:
The American Youth Horse Council
4093 Ironworks Pike
Lexington, KY 40511

1-800-Try-AYHC (They publish a horse industry handbook. Call or write for information.)

North American Riding for the Handicapped Association
P.O. Box 33150
Denver, CO 80233

American Horse Shows Association
220 E. 42nd St. Suite 409
New York, New York, 10017-5809

(They have a rider's guide. Write them for information.)

Birds

The Topography of a Bird

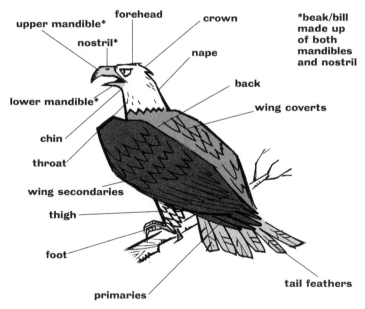

*beak/bill made up of both mandibles and nostril

- forehead
- crown
- upper mandible*
- nostril*
- nape
- back
- lower mandible*
- wing coverts
- chin
- throat
- wing secondaries
- thigh
- foot
- primaries
- tail feathers

Bird Nest Building Supply Co.

In the spring when the birds are nesting, here's how you can help them out:

Get a net bag, the kind oranges or onions come in, and fill it with different materials a bird might use for its nest—leaves, short lengths of string and yarn, hair, feathers, twigs, dried grass, straw, small scraps of cloth—use your imagination! Let the different materials stick out from the bag so the birds can get at them easily. Tie the bag to a tree branch; try to find a spot where you can observe the birds.

Other Animals

Top Three Low-Maintenance Pets

1. Hermit Crab: This wins the "Easiest Pet Award," hands-down. Hermit crabs make pretty dull companions, but the good news is, they're easy to take care of. They need food and water every now and then, but chances are, the water will evaporate before they drink it up. They eat just about anything, but you should probably give them official hermit crab food. How much they eat depends on how many and how big they are. Just check the food supply every few days, and feed them when their dish is empty.

Most exciting hermit crab activity: Males sometimes lose their claws when getting into fights with each other.

Hermit crab tricks: Eating.

2. Siamese Fighting Fish (also known as Rumblefish or Beta): These fish can go for days without food and if you feed them freeze-dried worm cubes, they'll go even longer. They don't need a fancy aquarium—a goldfish bowl works just fine. Their water should be changed every week or two. Don't buy two, though: there's a reason why they're called fighting fish. Females aren't as hardy as males, so pet stores sell only male Beta. If you put two males together, you'll end up with one dead fish—sometimes two.

Most exciting Siamese Fighting fish activity: fighting (if given a chance).

Siamese fighting fish tricks: The male makes a "bubble nest."

3. Hamster: This is the easiest of all the rodents. It needs water and food every few days and its cage can go several weeks between cleanings. Hamsters are furry and fun to hold. They like company, but be careful who you let in the cage with them: Two hamsters can turn into 16 in a very short time!

Most exciting hamster activity: Making more hamsters.

Hamster tricks: Running around on a treadmill; also, they'll let you dress them up as a bride and groom.

Receive a Free Animal Magazine

Best Friends magazine has stories, tips and information about all kinds of animals. To get it (and a brochure: "Careers Helping Animals") write to:

Nathania Gartman
P.O. Box 13
Kanub, VT 84741

Creature Catching

One of the best ways to learn about reptiles and amphibians is to "borrow" one for a while. But if you do, make sure you return it to its home in one piece. Also, don't be a homewrecker: leave your creature's habitat in the same condition you found it!

Catching Lizards: Lizards are cold-blooded, which means they need to be warmed by the sun before they can go about their lizard business. Their scales work like solar heating panels. When they bask, they're really collecting and storing solar energy, to use later.

Because lizards are sluggish in the morning, that's the best time to catch one. Move toward it very slowly, as it basks. Pick the lizard up by the back of its neck. If you grab a lizard by its tail, the tail will fall off and thrash around for several minutes.

This is a lizard's natural defense against its predators. Although lizards eventually grow a new tails, it's not a good idea to go around pulling off their tails—lizards are more vulnerable to predators (and less attractive to mates) without their tails.

Salamanders, Newts, and Efts: These creatures "drink" water by absorbing it through their porous skin. They need to stay in dark, moist places to survive. The best place to find one is under a log or the branch of a fallen tree. When you lift the log, be sure to replace it gently: a whole universe of creatures make its home in the decaying wood. Always wet your hand before picking up newts—your 98.6° dry hand feels like a hot oven to them. Also, don't hold on to them too long because they'll die if their skin dries out.

Capturing Tips

B ring a container with plenty of air holes. Once you get your new pets home, they'll need homes of their own. Glass terrariums (available at pet stores) can be adapted to whatever environment you need.

■ Salamanders require lots of water, some dry land, and some green plants.

■ Frogs, tadpoles and turtles should be in a semi-aquarium: lots of water, a little bit of land.

■ Snakes will need a cage.

■ Spiders are easy to catch.

What Do They Eat?

■ **Frogs, salamanders, and lizards:** Insects with soft bodies and very small worms

■ **Tadpoles:** Water plants and cornmeal

■ **Turtles:** Lettuce, worms, cut up or ground meat, fish

■ **Snakes:** Chopped up raw meat or fish, mice, and smallish eggs

■ **Spiders:** Bugs and flies

CATCHING A DOODLEBUG

Lots of insects make their homes in the ground. When they burrow they bring the displaced dirt up to the surface. If you look closely, you'll see the entrances to these underground tunnels; they look somewhat like miniature volcanoes. You can stick a long blade of grass down one of the volcano holes. Sometimes a lion beetle, or "doodlebug" will be clinging to the grass when you pull it back up! Study it for a bit, then let it go back home.

Warning: Some wasps burrow into the ground, too. Steer clear of them!

The Care and Feeding of A Venus Flytrap

Venus Flytraps (*Dionaea Muscipula*) are rare and endangered plants. Never buy one from anyone but an official carnivorous plant dealer, or a nursery. They only grow in one place on earth—the coastal plain of North and South Carolina. Their "traps" are a pair of hinged leaves which, when opened, lure insects with nectar. When an insect lands, the movement sends an electrical signal to the plant's central nervous system,  and the trap is sprung. If the insect is very small, it can escape through the Flytrap's intertwined "bars."

■ **Venus Flytraps are picky eaters:** If they don't like the taste of a particular insect, the trap opens, and the lucky bug is set free. When a large, tasty insect is trapped, it is slowly dissolved by the plant's digestive juices. It can take up to three weeks for a Venus Flytrap to "eat" an insect. Once the soft inside part of the bug is digested (the outer skeleton is left behind) the trap opens once more, and the plant waits for its next customer.

■ **Never use tap water** if you want to keep your Flytrap happy and healthy! The harsh chemicals in most tap water will eventually poison your plant. Pour a thin layer of distilled water into a shallow dish or tray and set your potted Flytrap in it. Allow the plant to dry out a little between waterings.

■ **Venus Flytraps flower in the spring,** and produce a rosette of small, flat traps. In the summer, larger traps are produced (the better to catch large bugs). During its growing season, *Dionaea muscipula* constantly produces new traps, as the old ones wither and turn black. The old traps should be trimmed from your plant. In the winter, the plant is semi-dormant and doesn't need to be fed. Leave it in a cool, dark place and keep it moist (but not soggy) until spring.

■ **One company that sells meat-eating plants** is Carnivorous Carnivores, which is run by Peter D'Amato and Marilee Maertz. Peter first got interested in carnivorous plants when he was ten years old. He never stopped being interested, and now he is one of the largest growers of carnivorous plants in the world. You can write to him at Carnivorous Carnivores, 7020 Trenton-Healdsburg Road, Forestville, California 95436. For $2.00 you'll receive a catalog and growing guide for Venus Flytraps, sundews, and many other carnivorous plants.

Be a Field Biologist

Biologists—scientists who study living organisms— are constantly learning new things about our environment. You can help them, by picking an area in your neighborhood (a park, a field, or a vacant lot) and becoming the world's greatest authority on that particular place. Begin by giving it a great name, if it doesn't already have one. Next, make a map. (See "Get the Lay of the Land," on pages 138–139.) Draw in all of the natural features (trees, creeks, hills and rock outcroppings) along with some of the man-made ones.

Keep a record. One of the most important things a scientist does is to make repeated experiments and keep a careful record of the results. For instance, you could do a study of the birds in your area. With a compass in one hand and a pen in the other, sit quietly in your study area and watch the flight-lines of passing birds for exactly one-half hour. Using a field guidebook, do your best to identify the species. After noting the date, time, temperature, and weather conditions of this particular observation, write down the direction they're flying, and keep notes on their behavior in your study area. Are they singing? Chasing after one another? Foraging for food? Once you have this info, the important thing is to repeat this same experiment at other times throughout the year. When you've collected a year's worth of data, you might want to contact your local Parks Department or Audubon Society. Chances are, someone will be interested in all your hard work. You can do these kinds of experiments observing plants, insects, or woodland mammals (squirrels, chipmunks, etc.). You can even observe the behavior of the humans who share this piece of ground.

You could become the world's greatest expert on your particular study spot. Someday, someone may want to build a brand new mall in your study area. Your research might be invaluable in helping people to make the best possible decisions. If you enjoy this kind of research, there are many exciting jobs—studying toucans in the Amazon Basin or polar bears in arctic Alaska—that could take you all over the world!

Get in touch with the National Geographic Society, National Audubon Society or your local department of Fish and Game.

Butterfly Farm

1. **Find a caterpillar.** Use an insect or butterfly book to identify it and find out what he/she eats. The bush or leaf you discovered your crawler on is a pretty big hint!

2. **Keep your caterpillar in a jar,** with a few small holes poked in the lid. Every day open the lid a couple of times and sprinkle water on the leaves to keep them moist. If the leaves start to whither, replace them. Also, lean a stick against the inside of the jar so the caterpillar can climb up it and, eventually, make a chrysalis.

3. **Once the caterpillar does make a chrysalis,** wait and watch. When the butterfly does emerge from the chrysalis, take a picture while it's drying its wings. Then let it go. Unless, of course, you want to mount your butterfly as part of a collection.

How to Make a Killing Jar

Not as cruel as it sounds, a killing jar is what lepidopterists (moth and butterfly enthusiasts) use to kill their specimens quickly and painlessly.

Put a few drops of ethyl acetate (available from a biological supply store) on a piece of cotton at the bottom of an airtight jar. Next, put a couple of layers of paper towels on top. Put the butterfly in the jar.

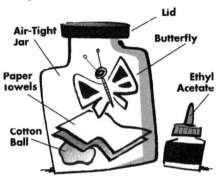

How to Mount a Butterfly

You can, of course, make your own display box, but you have to be absolutely certain it is pest free. If not, your specimens will be destroyed. Guaranteed-pest-free display cases can also be bought from biological supply stores.

Collecting Moths at Night

Do this on a night that's still (no wind), warm, and moonless.

Stretch a sheet out between two poles or over a clothes line—whatever's handy. Put a black light—not an ultraviolet light—in front of the sheet. Voilà—moths!

You can also raise moths in the same way you raise butterflies. Moth caterpillars turn into pupas, not chrysalises, though.

Worm Farm

First, you need to find a worm hole. Look for the little balls of dirt that worms leave on their holes. Dilute some dry mustard in water (not too much; you don't want to kill them) and pour it down the hole. Wait for the worm to wiggle up. Rinse the worm off, and put it in your worm farm.

How to Make the Farm: You should have a large plastic container (like the kind sweaters are stored in). Fill it with rich soil. You want to keep the soil moist, but not too wet. Every few days, put in a few large lettuce leaves and spray the leaves with water. Cover the box with a lid that has some holes in it. Worms are actually pretty fun to keep. They have lots of baby worms, and they're fun to see.

WORM FACT #1

It's true that a single worm can be male and female, but they *still* need another worm to have babies.

Homemade Ant Farm

You'll need about 100 ants, a one-quart mason jar, a shallow soup-sized bowl, and a pie tin that's bigger than the soup bowl.

Fill the jar and the bowl both about three-quarters full (no more!) with dirt. Put the jar in the bowl and the bowl in the pie tin. Fill the pie tin with water. The water will work like a moat to keep the ants from leaving the farm.

Don't cover the jar.

Feed your ants soft fruit dipped in honey or sugary water, candy, cheese, bread, vegetables—even bits of meat. Make sure you vary their diet. Keep the pieces of food small and don't let them get moldy—take them out if that happens.

Every couple of days or so, add a spoonful of sugar water to the dirt. Don't give the ants too much water, though!

You should see your first tunnels after a few days.

GATHERING ANTS

Look for small mounds of dry soil or sand—ants should be nearby. When you see an ant, hold out a pencil or stick. Let the ant crawl onto it and then gently tap the ant into your dirt-filled jar.

Worker ants live about six weeks, so that's how long you can hope to keep your farm going—unless you're lucky enough to get a queen!

Turn Your Thumb Green!

A Basic Vegetable Garden

You can give your family good food to eat all summer long if you plant a good vegetable garden.

Where: Vegetables need lots of sun, so pick a place that gets full sun for most of the day. If you can only get partial sunlight, it's better for it to be afternoon sun than morning sun.

Once you've decided where your garden is going, you'll need to think about what to plant. If you've got lots of sunlight and lots of space, you can plant big things like corn and pumpkins. If space is a problem, smaller plants, like carrots and radishes, might be better.

It's a good idea to plan your garden by first drawing a diagram. Mark off where you want each variety of plant to go and indicate where the sun will be passing in the summertime. This can help you get a better idea of what to plant. *Hint:* don't plant tall things like corn and beans in a place where they'll cast afternoon shadows over your other plants. Also, remember that gourds—like pumpkin and squash—take up lots of space, so don't put them in the middle of your garden.

When: It's best to prepare your garden after all chance of frost has passed. For people living in the north, this is usually in mid to late spring. Most seed packets have maps on the back that tell you when to plant.

How: The soil has hardened over the winter, so you'll need to turn it over, break up the clods and pick out any rocks. If you're using fertilizer to enrich the soil, this is the time to put it in. When you've finished working the soil, rake it smooth. Mark off rows for the seeds you'll be planting. (Some plants, like tomatoes and herbs, grow better if they go in the ground as seedlings rather than from seed. You can buy seedlings at a nursery.) Be sure to leave a small path between rows for later, when you'll be weeding and watering. Put empty seed packets on sticks to show what is planted in each row.

Next, make holes for your seeds to go in. Use your finger or a pointed stick. If you're putting in seedlings, use a small pointed shovel or a sturdy spoon. Once the seeds are in and well-covered, spray the entire area with a fine mist from your hose. Continue doing this each day, until the seeds have started to sprout and are firmly set in the ground. The soil around your seedlings should be damp but not soggy.

Weeding: Your rich soil will soon attract weeds. They are hardier than your seedlings, so you'll need to get rid of them as soon as possible. One way to discourage them from growing in the first place is to put wood chips around your plants. If this is too costly, though, you'll just have to weed, weed, weed.

Watering: If you live in a temperate area, you won't need to water every day. Just do it when the soil looks dry and the plants are starting to sag. Too much water is just as bad as not enough! The best time to water is in the early evening. Then, the water gets a chance to really soak into the ground.

How to Make a Scarecrow

- Nail two boards together in a cross shape, with one board much longer than the other.

- Get an old pair of pants and slip one leg through the long board. Put an old shirt on over the arms. Tuck the shirt inside the pants and tie them together with a rope.

- Stuff the body with leaves or straw.

- Stuff an old pillowcase for the head. Tie it off, stick it on the top of the pole, and tuck it into the shirt. Draw a face on with a marker. If you want to get fancy, you can sew on button features, but do that before you stick the head on the pole.

- Hats and gloves (stuff them!) are nice touches, but not necessary. If you tie tin pie plates on the arms the clatter might help to scare away the birds.

TO PLAN A FLOWER GARDEN . . .

Call Burpee Gardens (1-800-888-1447) and ask them to send you their free catalogue. They sell flower garden kits, which include a selection of seeds, plant markers, a garden plan and planting instructions. There are kits for sun-loving flowers, shade-loving flowers, perennials (plants that grow year after year) and annuals (plants that flower, then die over the winter).

A Forced Bulb

These are great gifts to make or sell in late winter, especially for moms, aunts, and grandmothers. Keep Mother's Day in mind, too. You'll need:

- Hyacinth bulbs—one for each gift. Buy your bulbs in the fall.

- A clear glass jar with an opening a little smaller than the width of your bulb. Dijon mustard jars are ideal.

- Ribbon

Buy your bulbs in the fall and keep them in a paper bag in the refrigerator until you're ready to start forcing them. It's called "forcing" because when you take your bulb out of the refrigerator, you trick it into thinking that spring has arrived. In nature, bulbs don't begin sending out roots until the ground thaws—usually in March. Bulbs need to "rest" for at least six weeks before they can send up new shoots. This resting time is called a *dormant* period.

Take the bulbs out three weeks to a month before you plan on giving or selling them. Fill the glass jar with water and place the bulb on top of it, with the root end down.

The root end looks a little bumpy, whereas the shoot end is pointed, like an onion—which is also a bulb.

The root buds should just touch the water. Put the bulb in a cool, dark place (not the refrigerator) and add a little water to the jar every day or so, to replace the water that evaporates. Once a week, change the water. Within a week you should see the root tips begin growing down. Soon you'll see a white shoot forcing its way up through the papery skin of the bulb.

When both the roots and the shoot are an inch long, move the bulb to a bright place—but not in direct sunlight. The white shoot will turn green and in a week or two you'll see a flower beginning to form inside its green tip. When the first bloom appears, tie a beautiful ribbon around the neck of the jar and give it to someone special. Everybody loves to get a living flower—especially when it reminds them that spring is just around the corner!

Forcing Fruits and Vegetables Is Fun, Too

Cut off the top of a carrot or pineapple and place it in a shallow dish with a little water. The leafy green part will begin to grow and your carrot or pineapple will start to send out roots. Change the water often to keep your plant from getting moldy.

More Growing Things

These make good gifts, too.

Re-Potted Herbs: At a nursery, buy a starter pack of different "kitchen" herbs—basil, thyme, rosemary, chives, oregano, mint, etc. Buy some 3" clay flowerpots and a small bag of soil. Take each plant out of its plastic cell and repot it into a clay flower pot. To repot, put a spoonful of soil in a flower pot, set the herb in the middle and fill in with more soil. Tie a ribbon around each plant, and give your herbs away as gifts.

An Herb Garden: Plant several different herbs together in a large round flowerpot or a small planter.

A Salad Garden: From a nursery, buy several different kinds of lettuce in starter packs. Put the lettuces together in a large flowerpot or small wooden box. Give with a bottle of gourmet salad dressing.

A Plant Kit: Put together a small flowerpot, a package of seeds and a Ziplok bag, filled with planting soil. Write growing instructions on an index or recipe card. Put your plant kit in a box, and wrap.

Re-Potted Plants and Plant Kits are great fund-raising items, too. Figure out the cost of each unit by adding up all your expenses and dividing that number by the total number of units. To get the selling price, double your cost.

Acknowledgments

Following is a list of the names of all the kids (and grown-ups) who gave us the stuff for both *A Boy's Guide to Life* and *The Girl's Guide to Life.* We are grateful to them all, each and every one.

If you know something fun or useful you think other boys ought to know, please send it to us. We'd like to include it—and your name—in our newsletter or in the next guide! Our address is:

Kids Life
116 West Jefferson St.
Mankato, KS 66956

Our phone number is (800) 394-4984.

Or you can visit us on the World Wide Web! Kids Life is at

http://www.kidslife.com

Thanks!

P.S.—If you've got a sister, she might like to read *A Girl's Guide to Life.* Just an idea.

Contributors

Brady Alexander
Cortney Alexander
Jazmin Alfonseca
Alex Anders
Marissa Arciola
Erica Arneson
Lauren Arneson
Mikal Baker
Arne Bakker
Philip Bannerman
Reuben Bannon
Gabriella Baum
Sabrina Baum
Drew H. Benton
Toby Black
Laura Blinkhorn
Susanna Bonam
Bonnie Bowser
Ashley Boyles
April R. Boyles
Brett Boyles
Denis Boyles
Evan Boyles
Hattie Boyles
Maggie Boyles
Marilyn Boyles

Nathan Boyles
Stuart Boyles
Travis Boyles
Whitney Boyles
Len Brantner
Ian Brodie
Dylan Brooks
Rebecca B. Brown
Sam Burrows
Ellis Caase
John Carlucci
Alonzo Carnozzo
Tessa Carnozzo
Larry Cassana
Penn Chamson
Andy Charlton
Sam Charlton
Christina Ciprian-Matthews
Dean Clayton
Amanda Clement
Bill Clifton
Pedar Craine
Jeremy Crouse
Elisa Dandrew
Miles Dandrew

Bob Davis
Lynda Deschler
Keith Dibert
Hank Dogget
Tom Downey
Stephen Duffy
Sarita Patrice Dunn
Ry Eiderman
Bill Englund
Shadisha Eubanks
Letizia Figg
Troy Figueroa
Dotsie Filanowska
F. Scott Fitzgerald
Joshua Force
Hillary Franck
Ursula Frenche
James Pierce Friedman
Charles Fry
Conor Gallagher
John Gallagher
Tavish Gallagher
Jake Gardner
Peter Garibaldi
Darren Garman
Marcus Garruba

Francesca Gioeli
Ryan Gioeli
Chelsea Gisando
Ajana Grantham
Aisha Gray
Melissa Guadalupe
Michelle Guadalupe
Greg Guttfield
Jason Hall
Terry Hall
Alan Hammer
Craig Hammer
Curtis Harper
Arno Harris
Ronell Henderson
Angelo Hennessey
Ariel Hensley
Max Hensley
Nathaniel Heubscher
Monk Hooper
Duke Hoover
Indiana Hoover
Texas Hoover
Olivia Horne
Frank Horvath
Jonas Howitte
David Donaghy Isler
Edmund Donaghy Isler
Tonya Israel
Karen Jameson
Ben Jervis
Charles Johannson
Georg Kajanus
Vinz Kamfritt
Megan Kelly
Susannah Kelly
Michael Kennedy
Johanna Kisimu
Peter Kunze
John Lardas
Lawrence Laskey
Stan Leach
Jeff Leader
Amie A. Lewis
Kevin Liang
Arye Lipman
Blaise Lipman
Danielle Litt
Kirsten Loderer
Heather Macrae
Kaitlin Macrae
Julia Madden
Melissa Magazine
Tristan Mantell-Hoffmann
Yves Manton
Jasmine Edith Marin
Fis Masterson
Norman Mazzarri

Charles McKinney
Patrice Metcalf-Putnam
Carly Moretti
Gillian Morgan
Honor Morgan
Andrew Morganstern
Tammy Mulford
Jordan Nassar
Jerry Neele
Max Newman
Rebecca Newman
Kris Ney
Alex Nixon
Marie Norris
Erin O'Brien
Wyatt Lowenstein O'Day
Hen O'Rourke
Natassia Ocasio
Frank Oliver
Richard Olivier
Steve Parin
Timothy Paterno
Brian Paul
Sanford Penn-Riles
Gary Pensance
Elvis Perrine
Caroline Pohlmann
Jon Robert Pohlmann
Rosina Pohlmann
Susan Pohlmann
Nora Prentice
Megan Raelson
Joey Randazzo
Madeline Weiss Randazzo
Curtis Reinking
Ethan Reinking
Joshua Reinking
Andy Renwick
Phil Rizzuto
Devan Robbins
Kelly Rodriques
Morgan Ross
Noah Ross
Nicole Ross
Sarah Ruane
Charles Ryland
Gretchen Salisbury
Yvette Sallay
Will Samuelson
Jackson Sansoucie
Kaitlin Sansoucie
Artemis Seay
Hector Seay
Elaine Seggerman
Jeffrey Shane
Daniel Shaw
Michael Shayne

Stuart Sherwin
Ajit Singh
Angela Sinicropi
Jamie Stack
Karen Stack
Suzanna Stack
Tim Stanton
Alice Starr
Benjamin Starr
Lisa Starr
Gregg Stebben
Peter Steers
Charlie Stein
Harry Stein
Sadie Stein
Hallie Steiner
Banner Stephens
Dan Stephens
Lenny Stetler
Elizabeth Stotler-Turner
Reuvie Sunshine
Hannah Sunshne
Tom Szody
Martin Takigawa
Chas Taylor
Matt Taylor
Sam Taylor
Shawnna Thomas
Matthew Torres
Alexandra Townsend
Rachel Townsend
Scott Townsend
Kathy Traynor
John Tubb-Tasker
Larry Turner
Priscilla Turner
Whitney Turner
Mark Twain
Philip Tzevelis
Rand Ulrich
Selino Valdes
Catherine Vasserman
Lucy Vasserman
Aili Venho
Clifford Venho
Mollie Vosick-Levinson
Simon Vozick-Levinson
Siddequa Walker
David Weir
Gregory Weir
Jonah White
Steve Wiener
Jamal Wilkes
Dave Wilson
Anna Zamm
Tim Zimmer
Dave Zincko